AMERICAN MERCHANT SEAMEN OF THE EARLY NINETEENTH CENTURY: A RESEARCHER'S GUIDE

ANNE MORDDEL

© 2020 Anne Morddel. All rights reserved.

No part of this publication may be reproduced or transmitted in any form or by any means, electronic or mechanical, including photocopy, recording, or any information storage and retrieval system, without permission in writing from the author.

First published in 2020 by Anne Morddel
Suggested cataloguing:

Morddel, Anne
American Merchant Seamen of the Early Nineteenth Century, a Researcher's Guide

Summary: Research skills using archival materials online and within archives facilities in the United States, France, Britain and elsewhere to find records on American merchant seamen of the early nineteenth century.

[1. Merchant marine—United States—History—19th century. 2. Sailors—United States—19th century. 3. United States—History--War of 1812—Merchant marine.]
I. Title

ISBN 979-10-96085-09-5

To my children

ACKNOWLEDGEMENTS

The Case Study, "A Seaman from Marblehead, Captured on a French Privateer, Joins the Royal Navy", first appeared, in an earlier version, in the April-June 2018 issue of the *National Genealogical Society Magazine* (volume 44 number 2) and is used here with the kind permission of the editors.

The Case Study, "A Nantucket Whaler Dies in a French Prison", first appeared, in an earlier version, in the February 2018 issue of *The Bunker Banner* (issue number 182) and is used here with the kind permission of the editors.

Much of the research in the British archival records on the Royal Navy career of Ambrose Dodd, for the Case Study, "A Seaman from Marblehead, Captured on a French Privateer, Joins the Royal Navy", was generously contributed by Dr. Brian Cooper.

I am most grateful to all of the above for their editorial suggestions and permissions.

TABLE OF CONTENTS

Introduction	1
Historical Setting	
A Time of Wars	3
Vessels in War	5
Follow the Vessel, Look for The Man	9
Documentation and Archives	18
American Documentation	19
French Documentation	39
British Documentation	63
Conclusion	79
Case Studies	
A Seaman from Marblehead, Captured on a French Privateer, Joins the Royal Navy	80
A Nantucket Whaler Dies in a French Prison	87
Selected Bibliography	93
Acronyms	97

INTRODUCTION

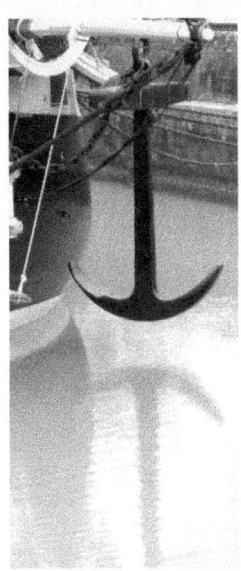

Documenting American merchant seamen of the first twenty or thirty years of the nineteenth century is quite difficult. Most American merchant vessels of the era did not carry crew lists and, where they did, few were preserved. Aside from the Seaman's Protection Certificate (which carries a description of the man but little more), and basic vessel registration, the records in American archives concerning this generation of merchant seamen are limited, yet further documentation exists elsewhere on many of these men. When something went wrong with a voyage (and things often went wrong), or a seaman got into trouble (as often was the case), someone, somewhere, usually wrote it down. When a vessel was wrecked, captured, or stopped at sea, details of the event often were recorded. When a seaman was taken prisoner or died in hospital or married, in many cases it was recorded. When a shipmaster made a protest to a consul or a sea report to a port authority, it was written and may have survived.

During wartime, people increased their documentation of events. From 1803 to 1815, most of Europe was at war. Napoleon and the allies of France fought Britain and the various allies in the coalitions on the Continent and at sea. Toward the end of this period, the United States was at war with Great Britain. At the same time, and continuing for quite a while afterward, emerging South American countries were at war with Spain. Throughout it all, American merchant vessels and privateers wove between blockades, disguised their nationality and tried to evade other countries' privateers in order to trade with and profit from all belligerents. Much of this activity was documented and the records can be found in American, British, European and Caribbean archives of the Napoleonic Wars and of the War of 1812.

The documentation is not as simple to locate and use as it would be if a seaman were a sailor in the United States Navy, where one could search for his name in orderly naval records or pension lists. When his work was mercantile, his activity may have been recorded in records of commerce; when he may have been distressed or in need, his case may have been discussed in consular correspondence; if he were on a vessel that was captured by a belligerent, his name may have been added to a list of military prisoners of war. Dedicated sleuthing and imagination are required to find and search through all possibilities.

Some of the records and archives explained in this booklet are online, but most are not. However, archival finding aids generally are online and, using them to identify a likely record of a man, one can then order copies of the documents needed. British archives tend to send paper copies in the post, while French and American archives tend to send digitized copies by e-mail. To do this research, one will need not only access to the Internet, but an ability to read a bit of French (or the language of whatever country's archives one is using), to decipher nineteenth century handwriting, and to be patient. The result may well be the discovery that a mariner was not "lost at sea" but had an extraordinary and documented life.

HISTORICAL SETTING

A TIME OF WARS

This period was a time of war for much of Europe and the Americas, many of the conflicts concurrent.

- **American Revolution 1776-1783** - between the American colonists and Great Britain
- **French Revolution 1789-1799** - a French civil war and including the War in the Vendée and the Terror
- **Haitian Revolution 1791-1804** - a Haitian slave uprising against French colonists and France
- **French Revolutionary Wars 1792-1802** - between France and the rest of Europe and Great Britain
- **Quasi-War 1798-1800** – an undeclared war at sea between France and the newly formed United States

In Europe, there was a year or so of peace in 1802, when the Treaty of Amiens was in effect, then war broke out again between France and Britain.

- **Napoleonic Wars 1803-1815**, during which the United States was neutral and trying to profit from the conflict. In the fight against Napoleonic France, Britain expanded the Royal Navy, making it an unparalleled naval power, but one that was always hungry for men to operate the vessels. The constant need for more men resulted in the use of press gangs on shore and in impressment at sea. So many Americans were impressed and forced to work on Royal Navy ships that this was one of the main causes of the War of 1812.
- **War of 1812,** between the United States and Great Britain, which lasted from 1812 to early 1815, and which was so overshadowed in Europe by the immense war against Napoleon that, to this day, many British and Europeans do not know that it happened.
- **South American Wars of Independence 1808-1833**, between the colonies in South America and Spain or Portugal, these wars were, in many ways, sparked by the earlier American and French revolutions and by the Napoleonic conquests of the Iberian colonial powers, and were at their peak after the Napoleonic Wars ended.

During all of these wars, American merchant seamen could be found on vessels of all nationalities and types. Merchant ships of European nations as well as of South American nationalities included Americans on their crew lists. American merchants traded with belligerents on all sides and their merchant fleet grew to be quite large, sailing to all Atlantic ports, where shipmasters often stranded seamen, leaving them to seek work on any vessel that would have them. Primarily during the War of 1812, American privateers with mostly American crews attacked merchant vessels of enemy nationalities, e.g. Britain and her allies. American whaling vessels, based not only in Nantucket and Halifax but in France and then in Britain, operated in Northern and Southern Atlantic whale fishing grounds.

VESSELS IN WAR

Some knowledge of shipping and naval activity during these wars will help in knowing where to seek documentation on American mariners.

1776 to 1783

During the American Revolution, America's Continental Navy was small, with few ships, and relied heavily on French naval aid to win the Revolution. Both Britain and the United States authorized privateers to attack one another's merchant shipping. American seamen captured by the British were sent to prisons in England and Canada. Benjamin Franklin, ambassador to France, devised a plan to send out privateers manned by Americans from French ports to attack British shipping. His purpose was to take British prisoners who could then be exchanged for American prisoners of war in British prisons. On the whole, it was not very successful but the idea was not forgotten and was revived in the War of 1812.

1785 to 1794

During these years, there was no United States Navy. Hundreds of experienced seamen, lieutenants, navigators, ship's carpenters, sail makers, etc. who had been in the individual American state and the Continental navies, were out of work when the Revolution ended and the navies were disbanded. Consequently, many sought work on merchant vessels. Others, who saw themselves as career naval men and not merchant seamen, joined other naval forces, particularly those of France and Russia. Joshua Barney, hero of the American Revolution, left the United States in anger in 1794 because he felt that the position he was offered in the new United States Navy did not reflect or properly reward his talents and previous service. He joined the French navy and led a squadron in Saint Domingue (as Haiti was then known) to suppress the Haitian Revolution. He returned to the United States when the War of 1812 broke out. John Paul Jones, America's better known naval hero, left the United States to serve in both the French and Russian navies; he died in Paris a pauper.

1792 - 1815

This period includes the French Revolutionary Wars, the Quasi War, the Napoleonic Wars and the War of 1812. On land, armies clashed from Egypt to Denmark, from Michigan to Moscow. At sea, naval battles were fought in the Atlantic, the Caribbean, the Mediterranean, the North and the Baltic Seas, as well as on the Great Lakes. Early during this period, the French Navy was nearly destroyed, firstly by its own seamen joining the French Revolution and rising up against the mostly aristocratic officers, and secondly by the serious losses in the sea battles against the British, including:

- What the British term the "Glorious First of June" and the French call the "*Bataille du 13 prairial an II*" in 1794
- The surrender of the Mediterranean fleet to the British in 1794
- The naval Battle of the Nile in 1798
- The naval Battle of Trafalgar in 1805

After this, Britain's Royal Navy became the supreme naval power in the Atlantic, and impressed more seamen, including Americans, than ever before. A vast number of Royal Navy vessels patrolled the Atlantic, the North and the Caribbean Seas, accompanied and protected convoys of British merchant vessels as they sailed through dangerous waters, and grouped around French ports, especially Brest, in a blockade to prevent French vessels leaving. What remained of the French naval fleet was usually trapped at Brest by the blockade, with occasional, significant escapes.

In addition to naval and merchant activity, all belligerents sanctioned privateering and issued authorizing Letters of Marque to privateers. With its reduced navy trapped, France strongly encouraged privateering by its citizens against enemy vessels; it was both profitable and patriotic. French privateers were highly successful against British merchant vessels, and those of Britain's allies, including American vessels. French privateers sailed from any port on the French Atlantic coast, from Bayonne to Dunkirk, but especially from Brest and Saint Malo, and they included many American seamen on board.

During the Quasi-War, French vessels captured hundreds of American merchant vessels. France was furious that the United States refused to repay the costs of French military aid given during the American Revolution and also saw the Jay Treaty of 1795 with Britain as a betrayal of the trust formed during that war and of the Treaty of Amity that the United States had signed with France in 1778. Though France did not declare a war against the United States for treaty violations, one was waged against American commerce, and many of the American seamen from the captured vessels were taken to France and jailed.

All of these wars were also fought in the Caribbean, where some of the islands were colonies of various European countries and where American merchant vessels carried on a great deal of trade. The geography of those numerous islands, some with secretive ports where vessels could hide, and a few with very corrupt governors, facilitated a greater amount of privateering and outright piracy. There were also many slave trading vessels, voyaging the triangular route from West Africa to the Caribbean Islands to the United States. American vessels were captured by French privateers or stopped by Royal Navy ships that impressed her seamen, or were attacked and often burned or sunk by pirates based on a Caribbean island.

1808-1833

During the South American Wars of Independence, what were known in English as "insurgent privateers" sailed from South American and Caribbean ports and attacked Spanish and Portuguese vessels. After the end of the War of 1812, many of these privateers were owned and manned by Americans, and a large number were fitted out in Baltimore.

Thus, at any time in the late eighteenth and early nineteenth centuries, an American seaman could have, for example:

- Served as a young man in the Continental Navy
- After the end of the Revolution, worked on a New York vessel carrying grain to Liverpool
- Worked on an English vessel carrying iron to Boston
- Been on a vessel captured by a French privateer and taken into a French port
- Sent to a French prison
- Been released from a French prison temporarily to work on a French privateer
- Been on the prize crew of a vessel captured by a privateer that either arrived in port or was recaptured by the Royal Navy
- Sent to prison in England as a French or American prisoner of war
- Been released from a British prison in 1815, at the end of the War of 1812
- Gone on a cartel vessel from Britain to Baltimore or another American port
- Signed on to a Baltimore privateer bound for Buenos Aires
- Settled in another country or returned to the United States

How to find him?

FOLLOW THE VESSEL, LOOK FOR THE MAN

The documentation of any voyage is centered on the vessel. Two key points will always be the identifiers, with a third often included:

- the vessel's name
- the shipmaster's surname
- the vessel type

The vessel's name is the primary fact given on any file or dossier, in any newspaper announcement of arrivals or departures, in all vessel registrations, on all Letters of Marque. The shipmaster's or captain's surname always follows, unless, as may be the case with a wreck when all hands were lost, it may not be known. Commonly, but not always, the vessel type, such as brig, schooner, snow or frigate, will also be mentioned; if so, it usually appears before the vessel name. Thus "schooner, *Mary*, Carter" or just "*Mary*, Carter" will be all that appears for a merchant vessel in a shipping news list. "Brig, *Argus*, Decatur" may be all that appears concerning the file or some of the ordinary movements of a naval vessel.

Merchant vessels then, as now, were heavily documented. The ship's papers included the vessel registration, showing the nationality of the ship, the names and nationalities of the owners, the name and nationality of the captain or master, and a cargo manifest, showing the nation of origin as well as the owners of every bit of the cargo. Nationality was crucial to establish during these wars as it could determine whether a vessel were an enemy to be captured or a neutral trader to be allowed to continue her voyage. Those wishing to trade with the enemy or to sell enemy goods but also wishing to avoid capture and confiscation, often would supply their vessels with multiple complete sets of papers giving false registrations and nationalities while also carrying "false flags" of corresponding nationalities to hoist, even though this was illegal in all countries.

What were minimally documented, if at all, were the seaman. European powers, especially the French, had long required, by law, that all vessels carry complete crew lists. These gave, at the very least, the full name of each man, his place of birth, and his rank or position. British vessels also carried crew lists but present some difficulty where impressed American seamen are concerned. Royal Navy ships' muster lists often contain falsehoods about impressed American seamen. They may have been given false names, perhaps the name of a deceased, British crewmember, or they may have been registered under their own names but been given false, British birthplaces. (Where this was the case, African-American seamen were almost always given the false birthplace of what was then the British colony of Jamaica.) For much of this period, American merchant vessels carried no crew lists at all. It was, for a time, not required by American law to list the crew. The more unscrupulous shipmasters resisted crew lists, as not having them gave the masters the opportunity to abandon seamen in ports or to refuse to pay them at the end of a voyage. The crew lists that were made were a part of the ship's papers and were used to help determine the nationality of the vessel; in Europe, at least seventy-five per cent of a crew generally was required to be of the same nationality as was the vessel.

To find a seaman in a vessel's documentation, one must first know the vessel he was on. Without crew lists or any other documentation of his movements or career, this requires imagination and guesswork. It begins with knowing the likely port from which he sailed and the likely vessel on which he would have found work.

- **A naval vessel** - Many American seamen who became merchant seamen or captains began their careers in the Continental Navy. If on a British Royal Navy vessel, the merchant seaman was probably unwillingly on board, having been impressed. Recall that a seaman would not be found on a United States Navy vessel before the Navy's establishment in 1794. American seamen also were found, more rarely, on vessels of the French and Russian navies.

- **A merchant vessel** - This offered better pay than a naval vessel, but a much greater risk of being abandoned in a port far from home. Crews were smaller, food was marginally better, and voyages were shorter than naval cruises or patrols at remote stations. Merchant vessels plied all variations of the Atlantic trade routes between the United States, the Caribbean, Britain and Europe.
- **A slave trading vessel** - Some seamen refused to work these vessels and those who did work on slavers tended to do so exclusively. The most common route followed by American slave ships was the West Africa-Caribbean Islands-United States triangle. However, as the British continued to enforce their ban on slave trading, some American slavers also followed a route from West Africa to South Africa to South America.
- **A fishing or whaling vessel** - A fisherman was not a merchant seaman but at some point in a seaman's career, he may have been a whaler or fisherman. Fishing vessels sailed to the Grand Banks or in North American coastal waters; whaling vessels sailed to Greenland or to the South Seas whaling grounds off Brazil and Argentina.
- **A privateer**, a "private armed vessel" - Such a vessel operated legally only during a time of war and only with a Letter of Marque or commission from the government of the vessel's nationality. Privateers sailed on short cruises, generally of three to six months duration, attacking the merchant shipping of the enemy. Seamen usually jumped at the chance to sail on a privateer, for the opportunities for wealth were considerable and life on board was somewhat more democratic, though the life was also very dangerous.
- **A prize ship** – A prize vessel was a vessel that was captured by a privateer and that had to be taken in to a friendly port and sold. It was manned by a crew from the privateer, and captained by a "prize master".
- **A pirate ship** - Not very many seamen chose to work on a pirate ship as the life was so brutal and the risk of hanging, if captured, was so great. Pirate ships carried no papers and did

not maintain crew lists, so information about the men on them is severely limited, unless they were captured and taken prisoner or tried.

When looking for a vessel, recall the key points for its identification:

- The name of the vessel
- The name of the captain/master/shipmaster
- The type of vessel, e.g. brig, schooner, snow, sloop, frigate, etc.

The next details to seek about a vessel, and which help to differentiate it from others with the same name and type, or to differentiate voyages of the same vessel and captain, are:

- The port from which the vessel sailed and the port of destination, for any particular voyage
- The name of the owner

With this additional information, the mention of a vessel may give: "brig *Eliza*, Cooper, Antwerp" meaning that the brig *Eliza*, master Cooper, sailed from Antwerp.

On Which Ship Did a Seaman Sail?

It is rare that family stories or histories give the names of the vessels on which a seaman worked, nor are his voyages noted on his Seaman's Protection Certificate, if he had one. Finding him on a vessel involves narrowing the range of possibilities and then investigating the likely vessels. Start with the basic facts about a seaman, being his:

- Name
- Place of birth
- Date of birth

Most seamen from port cities went to sea quite young, at roughly the age of eleven to fifteen years. A boy as young as six, for example, almost certainly would not be found on a crew list unless he were accompanied by his father or a close male relative, who most likely would have been the shipmaster or captain. Seamen from inland towns tended to have been men who could not find work in their area and went to the ports seeking better opportunities, so such a man may not have gone on his first voyage until the age of twenty or even older. The awareness of these customs can be used to calculate from his year of birth the approximate years of a seaman's first or early voyages.

The closest port to where he was born is the likely departure place for his first voyage, but many seamen afterward sailed from the larger ports, such as New York, Boston, Baltimore or Charleston. If the seaman's parents' names are known, that may lead the research to a family shipping business. Many seamen began their careers as boys sailing on family-owned vessels. Godfathers, grandfathers or uncles who owned ships were often the first employers of a seaman and the port city that was the location of their business would have been the port of his first departure.

To find what vessel sailed on what date from which port, there are a few sources one might examine:

For American vessels

- Newspapers of the time, in the shipping news section, particularly *Niles' Weekly Register* (many copies of which can be found at www.hathitrust.org), give the departures and arrivals of hundreds of vessels for a port. Close to this section in many newspapers one can also find advertisements from ship-owners for cargo space. These often give the size and type of the vessel, as well as the master's name, the owner's name and such details as the tonnage.

- For some privateers during the War of 1812, the applications and requests for Letters of Marque can be found in the *War of 1812 Papers, 1789-1815* in the series "Letters Received Concerning Letters of Marque, 1812-14" (NARA microfilm M588). These are merely requests and may not have been granted. Moreover, they represent a fraction of the requests received and include none of the Letters of Marque awarded by United States Ministers to American privateers operating in foreign ports. Nevertheless, the information given is useful, including the vessel's name, owners, home port and, in some cases, the name of the shipmaster. This microfilm may be viewed online on either:

- o The Internet Archive, which charges no fee, but there is also no indexing of the film.
    (https://archive.org/details/warof1812paperso04unit)
- o Ancestry.com, which charges a fee and which has partially indexed some series in the papers.
    (https://www.ancestry.com/search/collections/1118/)

- The National Archives collection, "Records of the Bureau of Marine Inspection and Navigation" (Record Group 41) 1774-1973, is explained in detail in its "Guide to Federal Records". Most of this collection covers a later period but some is relevant and there are some crew lists. The guide is online but none of the records are.
  https://www.archives.gov/research/guide-fed-records/groups/041.html

- A second National Archives collection, "Records of the United States Customs Service" (Record Group 36) 1745-1997, also is covered in detail in the "Guide to Federal Records". The customs service controlled the departure and entry of goods and, consequently, a great deal of vessel information. Again, none of the records described is online.
  https://www.archives.gov/research/guide-fed-records/groups/036.html

- The Library of Congress Research Guide, "Ships and Ship Registers: Sources of Information" has an extensive list of resources, including "Databases and Internet Resources"
  https://guides.loc.gov/ship-registers

For French vessels

There is no list certain to have all of the French Navy, the *Marine,* vessels' names. There are better lists of French privateers but even these are not complete.

Perhaps the best sources on identifying the naval vessels of this period are:

- *Dictionnaire des bâtiments de la flotte de guerre française de Colbert à nos jours, 1671 – 1870,* two volumes, by Jean-

Michel Roche, published in 2005 by Group Retozel-Maury Millau.
- *La Marine du Consulat et du Premier Empire: nomenclature des navires français de 1800 à 1815*, by Alain Demerliac, published in 2003. This is a printout of a database.
- *French Warships in the Age of Sail 1786-1861 : Design, Construction, Careers and Fates* by Rif Winfield and Stephen S. Roberts; published in 2015 by Seaforth Publishing.
- The French language Wikipedia has a quite good list of French naval vessels: https://fr.wikipedia.org/wiki/Liste_des_vaisseaux_français
- A partial list, filled with question marks, can be found on a blog post, entitled "*Les frégates de la Marine française sous la Révolution et l'Empire, 1789-1815*" which is on the blog "*Les armées de ligne de la Révolution*" of the *Association société d'études historiques révolutionnaires et impériales* (SEHRI) (https://revolutionsehri.wordpress.com/category/fregate-de-la-marine-de-la-revolution-et-lempire/)
- The *Gazette nationale ou le Moniteur Universel* (1789-1810), contains numerous mentions of French vessels of all types, of actions and prizes taken, as well as of wrecks. Over 40,000 issues may be viewed and searched on Gallica, the website of the *Bibliothèque national de France*. (www.gallica.bnf.fr)

For Royal Navy vessels

- *The Naval Chronicle*. Published from 1799 to 1818. Digitized volumes can be found on numerous websites, including the Internet Archive and Hathi Trust. This covers the Royal Navy and gives accounts of captures, actions, wrecks, etc.
- *Lloyd's List,* described on www.maritimearchives.co.uk, and digitized on Hathi Trust, was a newspaper produced by the insurer and dedicated exclusively to shipping news and information.
- *British Warships in the Age of Sail, 1793-1817 : Design, Construction, Careers and Fates* by Rif Winfield; published in 2005 by Seaforth Publishing.
- *Naval History during the Napoleonic Wars and afterwards (1793-1827)* a category on the superb and massive website of Paul Benyon, *Naval Social History - Circa 1793 - 1920+*. https://sites.rootsweb.com/~pbtyc/Naval.html

For all vessels

- Know that any of the above can help to find vessels of more than one nationality. The vessel of one nationality may have captured, been captured by or fought with or rescued the crew of a vessel of another nationality, and that may be mentioned.
- The Ship Index (www.shipindex.org) The most comprehensive online list of references to vessels; it can be searched by ship name only.
- The Trans-Atlantic Slave Trade Database (https://www.slavevoyages.org/voyage/database)
- The Sound Toll Registers, in the Danish National Archives, are a record of every vessel that sailed in or out of the Baltic Sea from 1497 to 1857. A Dutch university has indexed them in two databases that can be searched online. Database 1 contains information on passages prior to 1634, while Database 2 contains information on all those after 1633. It is Database 2 that reveals some American vessels and shipmaster's names of the early nineteenth century. (http://www.soundtoll.nl/index.php/en/onderzoek/zoeken-in-de-sonttol-database)
- Continue to search online the finding aids of archives, libraries and museums, which often contain long lists of vessels. This is especially so in the donated papers of the large, ship-owning businesses or families.
- Continue to do broad Internet searches. Use different browsers, as they can bring up differing results on the same words searched: Google Chrome, Bing, Duck Duck Go, Safari, Firefox, etc.
- There are thousands of books and websites dedicated to the age of sail; any one of them could have information on a particular vessel.

Note every detail found, as each can be helpful in identifying a specific vessel. With an idea of his vessel and its voyages, one can look deeper into the archives of the places where a merchant seaman sailed, seeking documentation on him. Even a list of only likely vessels and voyages, based on departures from the port or ports closest to the place of birth, will be a useful guide during the search.

DOCUMENTATION AND ARCHIVES

An American merchant seaman who never advanced to mate or master, never was impressed, never was on a ship that was captured, never married, or did not die outside of the United States will be very hard, indeed, to document. However, for the seaman who became a master or was impressed or was on a vessel that was captured or who married or died in Europe, there may well be mentions, documents, even whole files about him.

The main geographical areas for archival research on American mariners during the Napoleonic Wars are:

- The United States of America
- The European countries to which the mariner may have sailed. France is the example here but the research concepts apply just as easily to other European countries such as Norway, The Netherlands, Portugal or Spain.
- Great Britain

AMERICAN DOCUMENTATION

"THE WATER FRONT OF A GREAT SEAPORT LIKE NEW YORK" [1]

The documentation in the United States can be divided into two types: those collections which deal with seamen generally (records about impressment and Seaman's Protection Certificates) and those which are about other subjects, such as the vessels or the owners, but may contain information about individual seamen.

Records About Impressment and Impressed American Seamen

There is much documentation on American efforts to obtain the release, case by case, of American seamen impressed by the Royal Navy. The National Archives and Records Administration (NARA) has microfilmed much but by no means all of it.

- *Registers of Applications for the Release of Impressed Seamen, 1793-1802, and Related Indexes* (Roll M2025) "consists of four

---

[1] Abbot, Willis J., *American Merchant Ships and Sailors*. (New York : Dodd, Mead, 1902), 55, illustration. Digitized on the Internet archive. https://archive.org/details/americanmerchant00abboiala/page/84/mode/2up (Accessed 19 August 2020)

volumes of registers of applications for the release of impressed seamen, with related indexes."[2]

- *Miscellaneous Lists and Papers Regarding Impressed Seamen, 1796-1814* (Roll M1839) "consists of five sections (called "Targets"...); the subject categories and time periods covered by each Target overlap."[3]

Both of these microfilm rolls may be purchased or may be viewed at NARA centers. The lists are long and, for the most part, not indexed. They represent the various efforts to prove the American nationality the men taken. The information comes from protests, correspondence and registers. Captains were supposed to report any impressment in a protest made to one of the United States consuls in Great Britain. Seamen, if they could, wrote to a consul, pleading for help. These letters can reveal a great deal about a seaman, as he may have named his family members, his place of birth, his vessel and captain, and details of his impressment, all in an effort to prove his American nationality. The consuls maintained registers of the cases of the applications to the British Admiralty for a seaman's release. They are described more on the website of the National Archives, (www.archives.gov).

A quite large collection, the "Records of the London Consulate", comprising eleven bound volumes in Record Group 84, have not been microfilmed or indexed and are difficult to access. These volumes are described in some detail by Nathan Perl-Rosenthal as the records generated by the London Agency for Relief of Impressed Seamen. The volumes include the sailor's name and race, his place of origin, impressment history, evidence of citizenship submitted on his behalf by the Agency, and the outcome of the case.[4]

---

[2] "Records About Impressed Seamen, 1793-1814", The U.S. National Archives and Records Administration, 14 September 2017, https://www.archives.gov/research/military/war-of-1812/1812-discharge-certificates/impressed-seamen-1793-to-1814
[3] Ibid.
[4] Perl-Rosenthal, Nathan, *Citizen Sailors: Becoming American in the Age of Revolution* (Cambridge" Belknap Press, 2015), 277.

Lastly, once American impressed seamen on board Royal Navy vessels at the time learned that the United States had declared war against Great Britain on the 18th of June 1812, hundreds of them immediately stopped work. On the grounds that their countries were at war, they declared themselves prisoners of war and demanded that they be taken to prisons. Royal Navy vessels obliged and took them to the nearest prison or prison hulk, whether in Jamaica, Gibraltar, England or elsewhere. There, the Americans were imprisoned with compatriots: seamen captured from merchant vessels and privateers. The prison entry registers are discussed in British Documentation, below, but American records contain some prisoner exchange records and a few detailed letters from prisoners. These are found in:

- *War of 1812 Papers, 1789-1815 - Agreements for the exchange of prisoners of war, 1812, 1813.* NARA microfilm M588
- *War of 1812 Papers, 1789-1815 - Miscellaneous letters received concerning the release of prisoners, 1812-15.* NARA microfilm M588

This microfilm may be viewed online on either:

- The Internet Archive, which charges no fee, but there is no indexing of the film.
  (https://archive.org/details/warof1812paperso04unit)
- Ancestry.com, which charges a fee and which has partially indexed some series in the papers.
  (https://www.ancestry.com/search/collections/1118/)

Seaman's Protection Certificates

In a response to the incessant impressment of American seamen by the Royal Navy, the United States Congress authorized the creation and issuance of Seamen's Protection Certificates in 1796. The customs collectors of American ports issued the certificates, based on applications by and approved registration of merchant seamen. Native and naturalized citizenship both were accepted. The certificate gave the man's name, age, place of birth, and physical description.[5] Some

---

[5] Dixon, Ruth Priest, "Genealogical Fallout from the War of 1812", *Prologue Magazine* 24:1 (Spring 1992),

applications, but not certificates, may name the vessel on which the seaman found work. With the Seamen's Protection Certificates, the American consuls in Great Britain had a tool to help them in claims for an impressed seaman's release from a Royal Navy vessel, while seamen had something they valued enormously, believing it would protect them from being impressed. However, for a number of reasons, the certificates were not entirely reliable for either identification or proof of nationality. These reasons include:

- Once Seamen's Protection Certificates became accepted and common, foreign seamen began to acquire them in American ports, presumably as protection against impressment or military service.
- Some Americans acquired them in different names and carried two or three.
- Seamen sold their Seamen's Protection Certificates or, conversely, bought or stole them from someone else.
- When one seaman died, at sea or in prison, his effects were often sold; providing another seaman with the opportunity to buy or take his Seamen's Protection Certificate and other documents and work under the dead man's name.
- Among the double or even triple sets of ship's papers and flags that a vessel might have carried, false crew lists could vary the nationalities of the crewmembers, conflicting with the information on a Seamen's Protection Certificate, making identification and proof of nationality difficult.
- If a ship were stopped or captured, either captive or captor seamen might have thrown all documents, including the certificates, overboard.
- Those who impressed or imprisoned American seamen often destroyed their Seamen's Protection Certificates.
- When imprisoned, especially in Britain but also in France, American seamen seem, at times, to have traded round their documents before roll calls, apparently in order to confuse their captors as to their identities. [6]

---

https://www.archives.gov/publications/prologue/1992/spring/seamans-protection.html. [Accessed 29 September 2019]
[6] Morddel, Anne, "Resources for Tracing Impressed American Seamen." *NGS Magazine*, (44:2, April-June 2018), 30.

In spite of these drawbacks, the Seamen's Protection Certificates and the applications for and indices to them remain the primary American document to seek when researching a merchant seaman. Online indices to them can be found at the websites of:

- The Mystic Seaport Museum
  (https://research.mysticseaport.org/databases/protection/)

  There are entries for 30,988 certificates issued from 1796-1871 by the customs collector of Fall River, Gloucester, New Haven, New London, Newport, Marblehead, and Salem.[7]

- Ancestry

  Indexes to Seamen's Protection Certificate Applications and Proofs of Citizenship
  (https://www.ancestry.com/search/collections/49193/)

  Register of Seamen's Protection Certificates from the Providence, Rhode Island Customs District, 1796-1870
  (https://www.ancestry.com/search/collections/49313/)

  U.S., Citizenship Affidavits of US-born Seamen at Select Ports, 1792-1869
  (https://www.ancestry.com/search/collections/1928/)

  "The three volumes make available to researchers a user-friendly finding aide to the names of almost 50,000 seamen who filed for a Seaman's Protection Certificate between 1796 and 1861 in 13 East Coast and Gulf of Mexico ports. This index covers a dozen ports with from 4,400 applications for the Port of New Orleans to 18 proofs of citizenship for the Port of New London, Connecticut. The two previous indexes were to 33,000 applications field in the Port of Philadelphia. Some of these records are in excellent condition; however, some suffer from neglect, and many are missing."[8]

---

[7] "Registers of Seamen's Protection Certificates", https://research.mysticseaport.org/databases/protection/
[8] "About Indexes to Seamen's Protection Certificate Applications and Proofs of Citizenship". [quoting Ruth Dixon Priest] Ancestry.com.

Kathleen Brandt, in her article for www.archives.com on impressment adds further collections, of which these relate to the first years of the nineteenth century:

- *Proofs of Citizenship Used To Apply For Seamen's Protection Certificates for the Port of New Orleans, Louisiana,* 1800, 1802, 1804-1812, 1814-1816, 1818-1819, 1821, 1850-1851, 1855-1857 NARA microfilm publication M1826.
- *Proofs of Citizenship Used to Apply for Seamen's Certificates for the Port of Philadelphia, Pennsylvania,* 1792-1861. NARA microfilm M1880."[9]
 These may be viewed on FamilySearch:
 https://www.familysearch.org/search/collection/2290427?collectionNameFilter=true

The customs officials did not keep copies of the Seamen's Protection Certificates and few of the original documents, carried by the seamen, have survived. There are some examples on the websites of Mystic Seaport and other museums and they occasionally can be found for sale on auction websites.

We are often trapped into thinking that what is available easily is all that is available. This mistake leads many people to think that the only useful American records on seamen are the Seamen's Protection Certificates, but there is much, much more.

Ships' Papers or Maritime Documents

The most complete discussion, with excellent photographs, of early American ships' papers is Douglas L. Stein's *American Maritime Documents, 1776-1860*. Most such documentation concerned the construction, registration, ownership, insurance and clearing of the vessel and the ownership, marks, customs clearance and insurance of the cargo. Nearly all will mention either the owner's or the

---

https://www.ancestry.com/search/collections/49193/ [Accessed 22 August 2020]

[9] Brandt, Kathleen, "Researching Your 1812 Impressed Seamen," 10 July 2012, *Archives.com* (http://www.archives.com/experts/brandt-kathleen/1812-impressed-seamen.html).

shipmaster's names. The few among the many types of ships' papers, in addition to the crew list, that may name a seaman were:

- Passenger Lists – Especially on return voyages, a seaman may appear as a passenger. He would not have been hired but was allowed to work his way home.
- Articles of Agreement or Crew Agreement – This was a document required for every vessel sailing from the United States to a foreign port and for certain other vessels; it was signed by the shipmaster and by every member of the crew.
- Ships' Logbooks - Many of these are published online by museums and archives. Occasionally, they give the names of crew members.

Some American institutions with large collections of early nineteenth century log books and ships' papers are:
- Mystic Seaport Museum
- Phillips Library at the Peabody Essex Museum
- Chesapeake Bay Maritime Museum
- J. Welles Henderson Research Center at the Independence Seaport Museum
- Library of Congress
- Smithsonian Museum
- National Archives Regional Centers

Though a Canadian website and though the documentation covers a later period, The Maritime History Archive has a most thorough discussion and explanation of Crew Agreements. (https://www.mun.ca/mha/mlc/index.php)

Individual ship's documents often turn up on auction websites.

Marine Society Archives and Membership Certificates

Salem, Philadelphia, Boston, Newburyport, Baltimore, Charleston and many other towns formed Marine Societies in the eighteenth century. Initially, they were formed to provide relief and aid to aged and indigent seamen and to widows and families of seamen.[10] Seamen who were members were issued with certificates. A few of these societies

---

[10] Stein, Douglas L., *American Maritime Documents, 1776-1860*, (Mystic Seaport : Mystic Seaport Museum, 1992), 108.

still exist and maintain websites and have published histories, with lists of early members.

- Marine Society of the City of New York –
  http://www.marinesocietyny.org/
  with its archives held at the Stephen B. Luce Library:
  https://sunymaritime.libguides.com/c.php?g=730491&p=5217808
- Boston Marine Society –
  https://www.bostonmarinesociety.org/
- Salem Marine Society –
  http://marinesocietysalem.org/home.html

As with ships' papers, individual membership certificates often turn up on auction websites.

Dispatches from United States Diplomatic Ministers and Consuls

From 1792, United States consuls were charged with aiding "distressed American seamen". Distress could have been caused by illness, indigence, imprisonment, impressment and, quite often, abandonment. The American consul or consular agent in a port was the first person the seaman would have tried to contact when he was in trouble. He would have had to prove his American nationality to the consul, and this might have been done with his Seaman's Protection Certificate, if he had one. If not, he would give details of his family and birth to prove his nationality. If a consul had doubts, he might have asked the seaman to describe the town he claimed was his home. Some or all of these details, or copies of his original letters, may survive in the consular dispatches. Consuls were also charged with reporting on American shipping in the ports where they were based.

Generally, diplomats (the Ministers Plenipotentiary to a country), left the aiding of seamen to the consuls but, at times, they became involved in a case. Much of their correspondence about such cases survives in the diplomatic dispatches. Both the series of the consular dispatches and of the diplomatic dispatches were microfilmed in the 1950s and now may be purchased in digitized format from the National Archives and Records Administration (NARA).

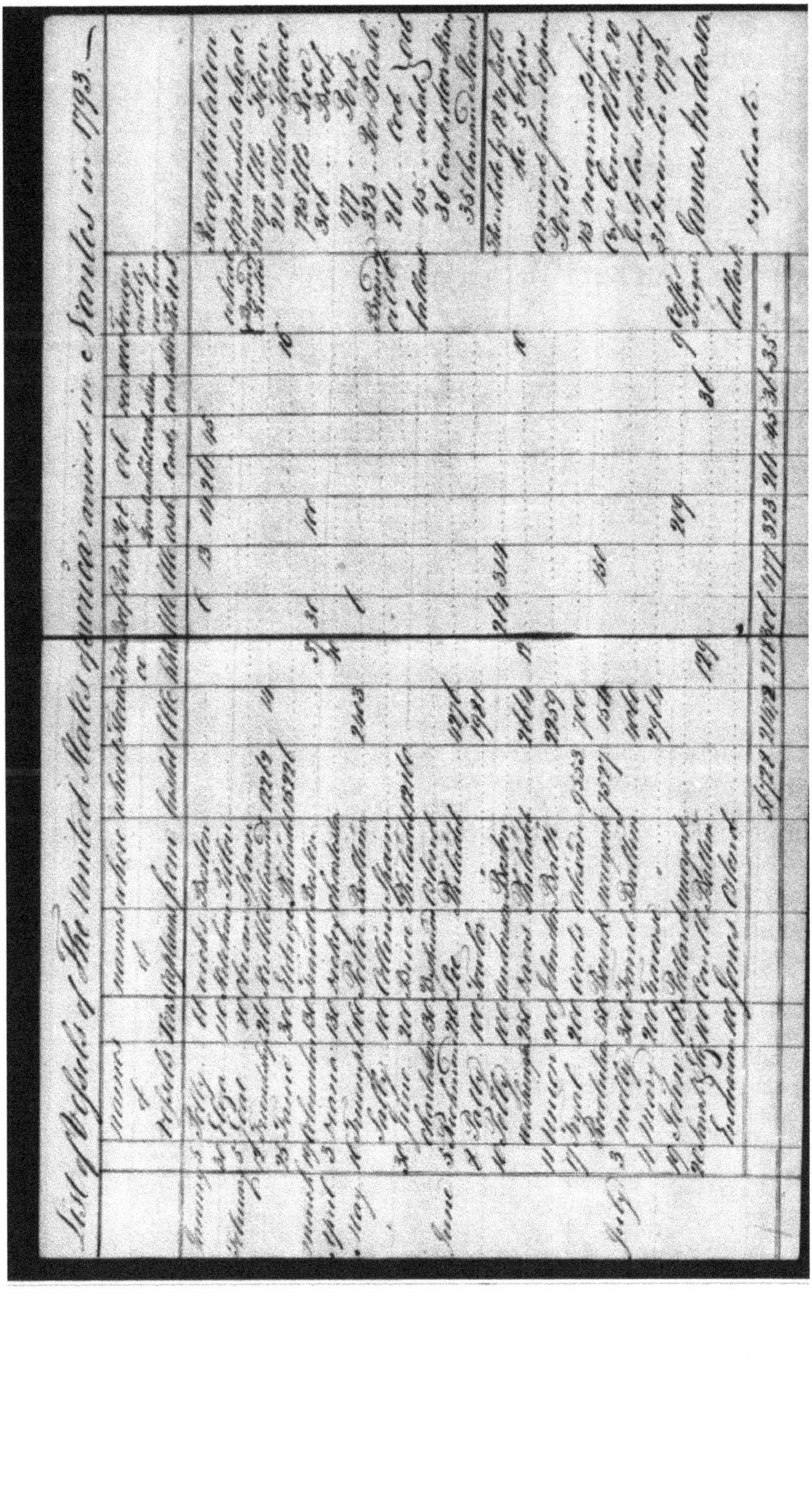

List of Vessels of The United States of America arrived in Naples in 1793. —

James Anderson

The above image[11] shows a typical consul's report on the American vessels that arrived in the port where he was based, in this case, Nantes, France. It covers the first six months of 1793 and gives:

- The name of the vessel
- The tonnage
- The name of the captain
- The port from which the vessel sailed
- The cargo

The first three entries show:

- On the 5th of January, the *Polly*, of 66 tons, Captain Wicks, arriving from Boston
- On the 30th of January, the *Eliza*, of 110 tons, Captain Hitchins, arriving from Pillou [possibly Pillau, now known as Baltiysk, in Russia]
- On the 5th of February, the *Goat*, of 80 tons, Captain O'Brien, arriving from an unnamed port in Spain.

Though a seaman's name will not appear on such a list, this kind of document can be of help in following his vessel.

Consular correspondence about specific distressed seamen can be incredibly revelatory about the man, as this unfortunately very faint example shows.

---

[11] U.S. Consul Nantes to U.S. Department of State, Letter, February 7, 1794; Vol. 1, October 7, 1790-July 8, 1850; Consular Correspondence, *Despatches from U.S. Consul in Nantes, 1790-1906*, (National Archives Microfilm Publication T223, roll 1); Record Group 59: General Records of the Department of State, U.S. National Archives.

C. M. Harrison Recd 26th

Saint Bartholomews
1st April 1791

Sir

In addition to the Letter, I have the honor to address to you of the 3rd ult. which has been detained here untill this moment; They leave to inform you of a transaction, accompanied by circumstances of such aggravated cruelty "as to call forth the indignant feelings of every individual to whom it was known:" And is as follows. About Ten days ago, "a party of Seamen left here in a small Sloop rigg'd boat to Join a Satrocl cruiser at Anabice in one of the out-bays, or Roadsteads, in view of this port, and as is generally the case, some of their former "Shipmates and friends accompanied them," amongst whom was a Mate by the name of John Beaven, a native of Warren Rhode-Island, and a steady orderly person for that class of people. On the arrival of the "party" at the place they expected to meet the Ship, they found she was gone; having been chased off by some French Men of War, that unexpectedly made their appearance in that vicinity": The day being now far advanced, and no prospect of "serving the Privateer, they began to feel the effects of hunger, and with the exceptions of Beaven, all landsmen, "& Sailor like" hav-
-ing

This is a letter[12] from R.M. Harrison, the consul in Saint Bartholomew (Saint Barthélémy), dated the 3rd of April 1821, discussing the case of an American seaman. In part, it reads:

> "...*a man by the name of John Bowen, a native of Warren Rhode Island and a steady orderly person for that class of people.....*"[seamen, as a "class of people" had a dreadful reputation]

In this and subsequent letters, the story is told that Bowen and a group of seamen had rowed out in a boat and tried to join a South American privateer then in the harbor but were "chased off by a French Man of War". They then found themselves far from the harbor and getting hungry. They rowed close to shore at a spot near a village and started shooting at goats for food. The outraged mayor of that village started shooting back at their boat, hitting Bowen in the hip. His comrades threw the badly injured Bowen on shore and sped away. Bowen managed to crawl to a street where he collapsed. He lay there, "without shelter or medical aid", for many hours until a former shipmate discovered him and organized help. A second letter from the consul to the Secretary of State about the case tells that Bowen lingered for two weeks and then died. If no letter to Bowen's family were sent or survived, if no one knew what happened to him, family records may say, at best, that he was "lost at sea". Here, his sad fate is given in full.

While United States consuls were constantly dealing with distressed seamen, they also were dealing with seamen and officers who were seeking work in foreign navies. They asked the consuls and/or the Ministers for introductions and assistance and the related correspondence can appear in the dispatches.

To find both diplomatic and consular dispatches, see the publication, "Diplomatic Records: A Select Catalog of National Archives

---

[12] U.S. Consul St. Bartholomew to U.S. Department of State, Letter, April 3, 1821; Vol. 1, June 30, 1799-October 28, 1828; Consular Correspondence, *Despatches from U.S. Consuls in St. Bartholomew, French West Indies, 1799-1899*, (National Archives Microfilm Publication M72, roll 1); Record Group 59: General Records of the Department of State, U.S. National Archives.

Microfilm Publications". This may be searched online at "The National Archives: Microfilm Catalog". Digital copies of the rolls may be ordered from NARA at: http://eservices.archives.gov. Sadly, they are not cheap.

Private Papers of United States Consuls

Many consuls' private papers and correspondence are preserved. In some cases, these contain more interesting correspondence than can be found in the official correspondence.

Sept.r — 20. Payé 1.o divers Dépenses au Sieur Demeur de Lorient pour la Canon

Logement Blanchissage de Linge et Alimens des Officiers durant les
Comptes Acquittés   ₶   ₶
Compte du Sieur Jean Jones ... 2.d Capitaine 491,25,
Id.m du Sieur Luis Cage Lieutenant 564,56, 1055,81,

20, Payé à divers Epicurs à la Dame Verdeur pour Anron

Logement &c.a des Suivants Marins après les comptes
au detail Acquittés savent

Compte du Thomas Read ... Maon 449,75,
Id.m de Rich.d Powell .... d.o 435,75,
Id.m de Will.m London .... d.o 453,25,
Id.m de Joseph Wilson .... d.o 416,25,
Id.m de Peter Schuler ... Cuismer 507,25,
Id.m de Domnych Schmelzy Apprentis ...... 440,75, 2,701,—

Payé au Sieur John Jones 2.d Capitaine pour Subvenu

The above image[13] shows a list of American seamen written in French and dated 1810 by the American consul in the French port of Lorient, Aaron Vail, to the French authorities; he sent this copy to the American chargé d'affairs in Paris, Jonathan Russell, and it survives in the latter's papers. The seamen had been on the crew of the vessel *Good Friends*, captain Winslow Harlow, of Philadelphia, when the vessel had been seized by the French. The mariners' names are listed, along with the amount of money Vail had advanced to them while they had been lingering in Lorient:

- Thomas Read, seaman
- Richard Powell, seaman
- William Tomlin, seaman
- Joseph Wilson, seamen
- Peter Steele, cook
- Vincent Ashmely, apprentice or ship's boy

The numerous claims by consuls to be reimbursed the funds they had advanced from their own pockets fill the consular dispatches and consuls' correspondence from most countries.

To find who was the consul for any given port during the early nineteenth century, look up the port on the website "Early American Foreign Service Database".
(http://www.eafsd.org/)

To find the private papers of a consul, use Google and a few other search engines with the following types of searches:

"[consul's name] private papers"
"[consul's name] family papers"
"[consul's name] archives"

It can be quite useful to search the consul's name both as given and in reverse, e.g. "Aaron Vail" and "Vail, Aaron".

---

[13] Brown University Library, John Hay Library, University Archives and Manuscripts, Jonathan Russell Papers, Series 2: Correspondence and Letters, Box 9; Aaron Vail folder, Brown University, Providence, RI.

A consul's or minister's papers may be found in the Library of Congress, in National or State Archives, in university libraries, in a museum or in a private archive. One must be prepared to enter into correspondence to request copies, if it is not possible to travel to do the research in the library or archive. Quite a few single letters from various collections have been digitized as a part of the two hundredth anniversary of the War of 1812, and these may turn up in a search.

Papers of the Secretaries of State

On occasion, letters from consuls about seamen and captains appear in the papers of the Secretary of State. Searching those online can yield a seaman's name, vessel and story.

James Madison from 1801 to 1809 (http://founders.archives.gov)
James Monroe from 1811 to 1817 (http://monroepapers.com/)

Prize Cases, or "libels"

During the era of privateering, a captured vessel was termed a "prize". It was taken into a port of the nationality of the privateer or to a port of an allied country. For the privateersmen, it was crucial to man the prize with their own men, called the "prize crew, headed by a "prize master", and to get it to a friendly port as fast as possible, not only to be able to sell the cargo before it might rot, if it were perishable, but to prevent the prize vessel being recaptured by an enemy vessel and taken home as her own prize. The original crew of the prize vessel became prisoners. When the prize crew took their places on their own vessel, they were moved to the privateer. At times, a very successful privateer would find itself bursting with prisoners, in which case, they might all have been put on the least valuable of the captured vessels and sent off home. Generally, however, the prisoners were brought in to port. In port, the prize would be judged as good or bad by a court. If it were judged a "good prize" the privateers and their backers kept the cargo and the vessel, and the prisoners were sent to prison camps; if a "bad prize", the vessel and/or its cargo, or compensation, were returned to the owners, and the prisoners released.

In the judgment of prize cases, senior officers of the both crews could have been interrogated, to know exactly what procedures were followed and when, and in what waters. Thus, a man who could have been a mate or a lieutenant on a privateer or a prize, may have given his testimony in a prize case. If a seaman was on a capturing or captured vessel that was judged in the United States, then it is always worthwhile to request the file of that prize case, or libel, from the NARA branch closest to the port where the case was tried. (For example, the files of the prize cases at the ports of Massachusetts are held at NARA Boston.) Most of these are not online; however, the War of 1812 prize case files for the Southern District of New York have been digitized and can be found on the website Fold3 at www.fold3.com.

To find out about prizes taken, while hunting a vessel that was either a privateer or a prize, know that:

- Reports of captures may be in newspapers, such as *Niles' Weekly Register* or *Lloyd's Register*
- Announcements of the upcoming sale of the prize vessel may be in local newspapers
- These reports and announcements reveal the location port where the vessel was taken and the case judged
- Occasionally, the finding aids of the archive facility holding the records of that port may list the vessels by name
- Mention must be made here of the impressive work by Greg H. Williams, *The French Assault on American Shipping, 1793–1813 A History and Comprehensive Record of Merchant Marine Losses* (Jefferson, North Carolina, and London : McFarland, 2009), which attempts to list and describe every case of an American vessel captured by the French during this period, through to the final resolution of claims. Unfortunately, it contains many errors.

United States District and Circuit Court Cases Involving Seamen

Crimes at sea were federal crimes and were handled by the district and circuit courts. A partial list of the types of crimes covered includes:

- Assault and battery [including on board a vessel]
- Evasion of customs duties
- Murder on the high seas
- Mutiny
- Piracy
- Slave trading
- Smuggling
- Unlawful fitting out of armed vessels [privateers][14]

Among these, one can find many cases of seamen taking shipmasters or shipowners to court for failure to pay wages, for brutality or for other complaints. Most of these court cases are not online, though very informative finding aids may be so or may be requested. For example, the plaintiffs' and defendants' names are given in full in the finding aids for the Massachusetts District Court Cases. The database entitled "U.S. Circuit Court Criminal Case Files, 1790-1871" on Ancestry.com "contains images of criminal case files of the U.S. Circuit Court for the:

- District of Maryland, 1795-1860
- Southern District of New York, 1790-1853
- Eastern District of Pennsylvania, 1791-1840
- Eastern District of Louisiana, New Orleans, 1870-1871"[15]

---

[14] "About U.S. Circuit Court Criminal Case Files, 1790-1871". Ancestry.com. https://www.ancestry.com/search/collections/1248/ [Accessed 22 August 2020]
[15] Ibid.

War of 1812 Pension Records

Nearly all of the War of 1812 records in United States archives concern men who were in the armed forces: militias, the Army, the Marines, the Navy, etc. and not merchant seamen, but for the significant exception of records concerning prisoners of war taken by the British (mentioned above and which will be discussed further below) and, to a much lesser extent, pension records.

From 1811, pensions were awarded firstly, to the families of men killed in action or who died while in service. Later, the criteria to qualify for a pension were expanded to include men who had been disabled by wounds received in service. As most merchant seamen were not, by definition, in military service, they did not qualify for a military pension. The sole exception was for the merchant seamen disabled while fighting an enemy vessel on an American privateer carrying an American Letter of Marque. It would have been very difficult for such a seaman to provide the documentation to prove his case but a small number did so and did receive their pension. Thus, it is worth examining the indices to the various pension records. Most of these are on Family Search:

> *United States War of 1812 Index to Pension Application Files, 1812–1910.* NARA microfilm publication M313 (https://www.familysearch.org/search/collection/1834325)

> *United States Old War Pension Index, 1815–1926,* NARA microfilm publication T316 (https://www.familysearch.org/search/collection/1979425)

> *United States Remarried Widows Index to Pension Applications,* NARA microfilm publication M1784 (https://familysearch.org/search/collection/1979426)

American War Memorials Overseas

https://www.uswarmemorials.org/index.php

Well over two hundred American prisoners of war, most of them merchant seamen, died at Dartmoor Prison in England. This website lists their names, dates of death, states of origin. It also has a list of the merchant vessels from which they were captured ut it contains a number of errors.

A number of books and articles have been written about Dartmoor and the "Dartmoor Massacre". The earliest is the compilation of memoirs of some of the prisoners, by Charles Anderson, entitled *The Prisoners' Memoirs or, Dartmoor Prison; containing a complete and impartial history of the entire captivity of the Americans in England*, etc., published in 1852. It can be read in its entirety on Hathi Trust:

https://catalog.hathitrust.org/Record/100259902

FRENCH DOCUMENTATION

As they were constant world travellers, early American merchant seamen's names can be found in documentation around the world. Because they worked on vessels of any nationality and sailed from and to any port, their names turn up in vessel documentation. Because seamen were often a troublesome lot, whatever their nationality and in whatever port, many were arrested and some records of such arrests survive. If they wished to travel on land, many countries required that people carry an internal passport and their requests for one have been preserved. Because Americans were often confused with British, they were locked up as British prisoners of war in France. If they escaped, a police bulletin describing them went out. If they decided to stay and settle, their marriages and the births of their children were recorded, as were the many deaths of American seamen.

Researchers using French documentation benefit from the fact that the French have been keen record keepers and archivists for centuries. Royal edicts and, later, laws of the Republic have mandated the maintaining of archives by *notaires*, by administrators, by clerics, by the military, by the legislature and by many others. While some archives have been destroyed by natural disasters or war, most survive and may be accessed freely (under certain conditions designed to protect the materials) by the public.

Passport Requests

During the Revolution and the First Empire, the movement of people was strictly controlled both within France and at the borders of the country, especially once the Revolutionary governments became stronger and were determined to stop emigration. Passports were not permanent documents of identification. They were single-page permissions for specific journeys and were to be signed by the authorities at each stop along the way. It is rare for the documents themselves to have survived. What can be found in the archives are the applications, sometimes with correspondence, or the administrative copies, falling into two main groups.

The first group is the passport request documentation, which varies greatly from one place to another. These requests were made to the *Police Générale* during the Revolutionary Period and through the end of the First Empire. They were not unique to French citizens because, at that time, everyone required permission to travel within the country. Thus, there are requests from Americans in France on business to go from Paris to a port, for example or, as another example, from shipmasters to go from a port, where their vessel had been taken as a prize, to Paris to attend the Prize Council.

PRÉFECTURE
des
DEUX-NÈTHES.

N° 3739

Anvers, le 21 Messidor an 13

II.e BUREAU.

Police

LE PRÉFET DU DÉPARTEMENT DES DEUX-NÈTHES,

A Monsieur Miot Conseiller d'État chargé du 2e arrondissement de la Police Générale de l'Empire.

Monsieur le Conseiller d'État

J'ai l'honneur de vous informer que le Sr Willet Smith, négociant américain s'est présenté devant moi, à l'effet d'obtenir l'autorisation de se rendre à Paris.

Cet étranger, arrivé à Anvers le 27 Prairial dernier sur le navire américain le Neptune venant de Philadelphie, n'était muni d'aucun passeport des autorités du lieu de son départ.

Le Commissaire des relations commerciales des États-Unis d'Amérique résidant en cette ville m'a offert de répondre pour lui. Cette considération m'a engagé à lui délivrer un—

In the above example[16], dated at Antwerp (at that time a part of the French First Empire), *21 Messidor An 13* (10 July 1805) the Prefect of the Department of Deux-Nèthes writes that Willet Smith, American businessman, arrived in Antwerp on 29 Prairial (18 June) on the American vessel *Neptune*, from Philadelphia, and wished to travel to Paris. The marginal note indicates that the request was approved and the permission document issued. Few of such requests from seamen seem to have survived but there are quite a number from shipmasters and captains.

The second type of passport record is a pre-printed register or log of all passports issued by towns or cities. These were in use mostly, but not exclusively, during the Terror, from roughly 1793 to 1795. In port cities, they contain the names of many American seamen.

---

[16] AN - Pierrefitte, F7, *Police générale-Demandes de Passeports, 1793-1818* [Police General – Passport requests, 1793-1818], Prefect of the Department of Deux-Nèthes to the Councilor of State, 10 July 1805, Letter. Photograph by the author.

N.° 1414 6°   N.° de l'état de popul^{on}.
du Registre.   Section d

Du 9 ξ C.ar an 10 de la République.

SIGNALEMENT DU PORTEUR.

Âgé de 22 ans
taille d'un mètre 714 millimètres.
cheveux et sourcils _châtains_
yeux _bleu_ nez _ordinaire_ front _étroit_ etc.
nez _Votais_ état _ras_
bouche _très_
menton _rond_
front _courert_
visage _ovale_

DÉLIVRÉ un passeport à _Isaiael Palmer natif des états-unis_ né à _Charleston_ département de _etrangers_ rue ____ domicilié à ____ département d ____ n.° ____ pour se rendre à _bordeaux ffr et_ ____ sur l'attestation des Citoyens ci-contre ____ domiciliés à Cherbourg, _à la lettre ou ____ du 9 soussignés. _nivôse an 10_

Le Maire de Cherbourg,
P.J Delariere

Signature du porteur du passeport.
Isaac Palmer

N.° 1417   N.° de l'état de popul^{on}.

SIGNALEMENT DU PORTEUR.

Above is an example[17] of the passport register book used in Cherbourg. There are three to four entries per page, all numbered. This one, entry no. 14146, dated *3 Prairial Year 10* (23 May 1802) gives quite a lot of detail about the seaman, Samuel Salmon:

- He was born in Charleston.
- He was a seaman in the United States of America
- He had arrived in Cherbourg from England
- He wished to travel to Bordeaux and had a letter from the prefect giving him permission to do so
- His physical description is given:
    - Aged 22
    - Height 1m 76cm
    - Eye color: grey-blue
    - Nose: pointed
    - Mouth: average
    - Chin: round
    - Forehead: low
    - Face shape: oval

On the lower left can be seen his signature. If a Seaman's Protection Certificate were found for him, this would allow for a comparison of the two physical descriptions to verify his identity.

Finding passport requests is aided by the fact that the indices to some are online.

- Those from the *Police Générale* (see the first example) are found in the *Archives nationales* at Pierrefitte. The entire name index is online on the search facility of the *Archives nationales*. (https://www.siv.archives-nationales.culture.gouv.fr/)

- Those from a city or town (see the second example) usually are found in the various Municipal Archives (the *Archives municipales*), of the cities. In some cases, they have been sent to the Departmental Archives, (the *Archives*

---

[17] AM Cherbourg, 4H2, *Passeports, 1793-5* [Passports, 1793-5] entry no. 14146. Photograph by the author.

départementales). A very few of these passport register books are online, on the websites of the individual Departmental Archives.

French Prize Records

As in America, the records of judgements on prizes (vessels captured by privateers or by naval vessels) and of law suits concerning those judgements were maintained. None of these is online. Worse, the archives of the central Prize Council, the *Conseil des Prises*, in Paris were completely destroyed in 1871 when the building was burnt during the rampages of the Paris Commune. However, in the *Archives nationales* and in some other archives around the country, many small collections of prize records survive. These follow the same pattern as United States prize case files and may include:

- Lists of captured crews
- Pay lists of privateer crews
- Prize court judgments (Recall that the judgment or decision as to the validity of the prize is crucial to determining the next step in researching a seaman who was on the crew of the captured vessel. Recall that, if the vessel were judged a "good" prize, the crew became prisoners of war; if judged to be not a valid prize, the crew were released.)

American seamen could be found on the crews of French privateers (as the example below shows) as well as on the crews of prizes, whether those vessels were of American, British or another nationality.

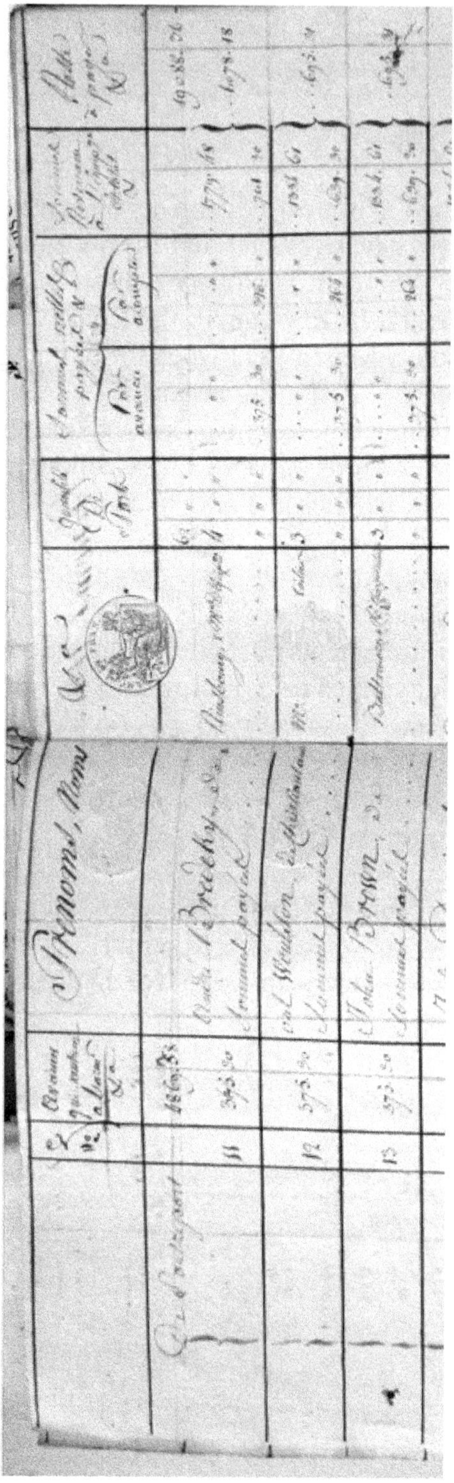

The *San Joseph* was a French privateer, operating out of the port of Saint-Malo in 1810. The image[18] above shows the first few names on the crew list and the prize money they received at the end of a "cruise". The third name on this page is that of John Brown, carpenter, of Baltimore. Further down the list, which runs to several pages, more American seamen may be seen.

---

[18] SHD Brest, 2Q/168, *Etat de répartition*, 1811[Pay muster for the *San Joseph*, 8 September 1810] Photograph by the author.

23	328.39	William Stewart, do Seaman, payat	Baltimore, ditto	2
24	328.39	David Wright, Do Seaman, ditto	Newyork, ditto	1
25	328.39	Richard Lee, De Boston Seaman, payat	do transporté	1
26	328.39	William Myatt, Seaman, payat	Baltimore	1
27	328.39	Edward Walters, 2 Seaman, payat	Baltimore	1
28	328.39	John Crocket, De Seaman, payat	Boston, ditto	1

The image[19] above shows five more Americans on the same pay list of the French privateer, *San Joseph*:

- William Steward, seaman, from Baltimore
- Daniel Schyes, seaman, from New York
- Richard Lee, seaman, from Boston
- Thomas Walters, seaman, from Baltimore
- John Tucker, seaman, from Boston

It is most likely that these men signed on willingly in Saint-Malo, where they may have left or been abandoned by a merchant vessel on which they had arrived. This exemplifies the free movement of seamen from one vessel to another. In researching a seaman, bear in mind that, if he has been traced to a merchant vessel that voyaged to one of the major privateering ports (such as Saint-Malo was) and then seems to disappear from the vessel, one reasonable place to look for him would be on a privateer sailing from that port at that time.

Finding French prize records requires significant sleuthing through archival finding aids. The main facility where such archives are held is the *Service Historique de la Défense* (SHD) in Vincennes. Prize records may also be found at the SHD branches at Brest, Cherbourg, Rochefort, Lorient, and Toulon. Some prize cases were judged by local courts and the records for these may be found in the *Archives départementales* of any of the departments along the Atlantic and Mediterranean coasts of France. A few records pertaining to prizes or privateers can be found in the National Archives of France, the *Archives nationales*. Most of what survive in these locations are lists and charts, not the depositions or decisions, but there are many names, especially in the pay lists.

At the time of this writing, no French prize records are online, nor are they indexed, nor is there a comprehensive summary of or guide to them all. However, there are a few websites maintained by passionate researchers that contain an enormous amount of information that they have extracted from original records or finding aids, or from books, or

---

[19] SHD Brest, 2Q/168, *Etat de répartition*, 1811 [Pay muster for the *San Joseph*, 8 September 1810] Photograph by the author.

from records that they have photographed. The best of these websites are:

- "War of 1812 – Privateers" (www.1812privateers.org)
- "Three Decks – Warships in the Age of Sail" (https://threedecks.org/)
- The Corsaires section of the web pages of Jean-Jacques Salein. (http://www.jjsalein.com/index.htm)
- The various corsaires pages on Migrations (http://www.migrations.fr/page%20d'accueil.htm)

Rapports de mer – Sea Reports or Captains' Reports

From the seventeenth through the nineteenth centuries, all captains or masters of vessels arriving in French ports were required to file a report on their voyage, called variously *Rapport de mer, Rapports de navigation* or *Rapports des capitaines*, telling of any incidents or encounters with ships at sea. They reported on news received from other vessels, sightings of privateers, actions witnessed, vessels in distress or abandoned, crew rescued, etc.. They are of great help in following a vessel.

The major Atlantic ports of France were Brest, Saint-Malo, Bordeaux, Nantes, Lorient, Rochefort, Morlaix, Cherbourg, Le Havre, Dunkirk, Boulogne-sur-Mer, Dieppe, and Calais. The *Rapports de mer* are in the *fonds de l'amirauté* (Admiralty archives) if prior to the French Revolution and afterward in the *Tribunal de Commerce* series or the *Marine* series in the relevant Departmental Archives. To date, only those for Nantes can be viewed online, and they include reports from a number of American captains.[20]

---

[20] AD Loire-Atlantique, 21U/457*; *Rapports des capitaines à l'Amirauté de Nantes* [Captains' Reports], (https://tinyurl.com/yd6ncytf)

Records of Prisoners of War in France

About 1500 American mariners were imprisoned with British mariners in France.[21] They arrived in ports on captured British ships and were marched to prison depots all over France, but mostly in the north and east. The French military and naval archives are filled with lists of these men, sometimes separated as Americans, sometimes jumbled with the British.

There are also individual dossiers maintained by the Ministry of War on prisoners who caught the administrators' attention for one reason or another. Most of these were British but there were quite a few dossiers about Americans amongst them. A complete list of the surnames of the prisoners (British and American) in these dossiers was published by the *Genealogists' Magazine*.[22]

---

[21] A database of these names is being developed by the author.
[22] Morddel, Anne, "English Prisoners of War of the First French Empire", *Genealogists' Magazine*, vol.30, no. 5, (March 2011), 153-160.

1807

Liste des américains détenus comme prisonniers de guerre au dépôt de Bordeaux qui ont été embarqués le 8 9bre pour être conduits à Anvers.

Noms & prénoms	Bâtimens sur lesquels ils ont été pris	Ports où ils ont été menés	Observations
Forges Christophe	perseverance	Bordeaux	
Bentley Rezr	Hebé	Dieppe	
Merry Benjamin	"	"	
Leprevost Job	Union	Bordeaux	

This 1807 sample[23] shows four mariners who were released from prison and sent to Antwerp to take a ship home. It gives their names, the vessels on which they were captured and the port to which the captured vessel was taken and where they arrived in France.

- Christopher Folger, of the *Perseveranc*e, taken to Bordeaux
- Kerr Berkley, of the *Hébé*, taken to Dieppe
- Benjamin Merry, of the *Hébé*, taken to Dieppe
- Job LeProvost, of the *Union*, taken to Bordeaux

The many lists of American prisoners are mingled with the lists of British prisoners of war in Series Yj in the *Service Historique de la Défense* at Vincennes.

Where an impressed American seaman was captured by the French from a Royal Navy vessel, his name may appear on lists of British prisoners; there, only his place of birth might reveal that he was American. The French lists of American prisoners are not online. However, the French lists of British prisoners were sent to the Admiralty in Great Britain and these now appear online in the "Prisoners Of War 1715-1945" section of FindMyPast.co.uk.. These are discussed in British documentation, below.

---

[23] SHD Vincennes, Yj29, *Prisonniers de guerre anglaise* [English prisoners of war] 1807, Transfer list. Photograph by the author.

Local Police Files

During the French Revolution, the Terror, the Revolutionary Wars and then the Napoleonic Wars, it was not rare for American seamen to appear in the local police files. Occasionally, this was because a seaman broke the law but more often it was, again, because he was thought to have been British and was under surveillance or on his way to a prison depot or had escaped from a prison depot.

When American seamen escaped from prison, they nearly always headed for the Atlantic coast, where they hoped to find a vessel to take them home. Local police files of coastal departments can contain the police bulletins sent round, sometimes with the names, ages and descriptions of the escapees.

Those Americans who were not arrested but were held under surveillance included artisans with skills valued by the French government and who were allowed to continue working, and American seamen who had just arrived on a prize vessel and were awaiting judgement of the prize. Most of the seamen were sent to a local jail, but some towns allowed them to live in town under police surveillance. The documentation for either situation may have survived.

Lorient, le 30 Juin 1810.

Monsieur et Cher Collègue

Plusieurs matelots provenant du navire Anglais l'Héroïne, capturé par la dame Ernouf, avaient été embarqués sur le Corsaire, en vertu de l'autorisation de Monsieur le Préfet du 3ème arrondissement Maritime et de celle de notre Collègue de Brest.

Le Corsaire étant venu de Concarneau à Lorient, quatre de ces Marins se sont rendus, dans l'espoir de gagner quelque port pour s'y embarquer sur un bâtiment neutre et repasser en Angleterre. J'en ai fait arrêter trois, qui vont être dirigés sur un des dépôts de l'intérieur. Le 4ème se nomme John Sharps natif de Baltimore. S'il se présentait dans votre port, je vous invite à le faire arrêter.

Agréez, Monsieur et Cher Collègue l'assurance de ma considération distinguée.

Le Commissaire Général de Police

A Mr. Le Commissaire Général de Police à La Rochelle.

The image[24] above is an example of an 1810 police circular about an escaped American seaman, written by the Police Commissioner of Lorient to the Police Commissioner of La Rochelle. He wrote that John Sharps, of Baltimore, who was captured when the ship *Heroine* was taken by the French privateer *La Dame Ernouf,* had escaped. More, Sharps was among a group of four seamen who, when captured, had joined the crew of *La Dame Ernouf* at Concarneau and sailed with her to Lorient, which is where they escaped, "in the hope of getting to a port where they could find a ship to take them to England". The other three men already had been recaptured, but Sharps was still on the run. The commissioner ended by asking that his colleague arrest John Sharps of Baltimore immediately, should he appear in his port. Probably, similar letters were written to other ports along France's Atlantic coast.

The details from this circular are:

- The name of the man: John Sharps [probably but not certainly "Sharp"]
- His place of origin: Baltimore
- His ship: the *Heroine*
- An approximate date of the ship's capture: June 1810
- The name of the capturing vessel: *La Dame Ernouf*

A quick bit of Internet searching on the names of the two vessels brings a contemporary newspaper announcement[25] on Google Books France:

---

[24] AD Charente-Maritime, 5M7, *Archives de la Police*, [Police Archives], Police Commissioner of Lorient to the Police Commissioner of La Rochelle, 30 June 1810, Letter. Photograph by the author.

[25] "Empire français", *Le Publiciste*, 25 February 1810, 3. (De l'Imprimerie de Meymat, rue des Moineaux, n° 423, Paris). https://tinyurl.com/y25snj3w (Accessed 12 February 2020)

Les deux prises faites & introduites par le corsaire *la Dame Ernouf*, capitaine Chabrié, de l'Orient, sont le trois mâts anglais *l'Héroïne*, allant d'Halifax à Londres, chargé de café, […], tabac, bois de teinture, essence & poisson sec ; & le [brick] *Maria*, allant de Cadix à Liverpool, chargé de laine, coton en laine, riz, tabac, raisin sec & vin de Xérès.

— Le 12 de ce mois, la cour de justice criminelle spéciale

It reported that Captain Chabrié in the *Dame Ernouf*, captured the *Heroine,* of three masts, on her voyage from Halifax to London with a cargo of coffee, tobacco, wood, dried fish and more. From this, the next research step might be to look at Halifax port departure records for more details about the *Heroine* and her crew.

Local police records are irregular but they are not difficult to find. There can be a great carton of them in some places and nothing at all in others. They can be found in two types of archives:

- Departmental Archives, in Series M
- Rarely, the local police records of the Municipal Archives of port cities can contain some interesting letters about seamen

None are found online. One must visit the archives facility or hire a researcher to do so.

French birth, marriage and death records

Some seamen stayed in countries where they landed and appear in registrations of marriages, their children's births, and in registrations of deaths. These, especially marriages, give much more information than in vital records in the United States or the parish marriage records of the same period in Great Britain.

L'AN mil huit cent neuf, le vingt quatre juillet
par-devant nous françois été adjoint ____ officier de l'état civil
de la commune de Roscoff _____ canton d'est St-pol de Leon
département du Finistère, sont comparus Robert Jean Marguerin
agé de vingt sept ans quatre [...] naissance [...]
de la Caroline Dusnord du amerique fils de defunts
Robert Jolson et de mary Brosshy cons qui est constaté par
acte de notorieté publique du 1er juin dernier devant le juge de paix de
[...] sous la date du 13 juin mil huit cent neuf [...] enregistré au bureau [...]
Le dit neuf du dit mois par quittet et [...] jugement [...]
extrait au Tribunal de [...] distance du dit St pol de Leon le vingt
six du ditcen [...] présidente [...] enregistré le vingt
trois juin présent au [...] [...] a Roscoff [...]
jusiez [...] vingt un ans et domicilié a Roscoff fils
de Nicolas thomas vichu et de Catherine [...]

jesquels nous ont requis de procéder à la célébration du Mariage pro-
jeté entr'eux, et dont les publications ont été faites devant la porte de
notre Maison Commune; savoir: les dimanches et [...]
[...] et date jullet [...]

The above example[26] shows the upper part of a marriage registration dated the 24th of July 1809, in Roscoff, Finistère. (A port favored by smugglers and privateers.) The groom was Robert Johnson, seaman, aged 27, of Newborn (New Bern?) North Carolina, the son of the late Robert Johnson and of Mary Brown. The bride was Suzanne Nicole Bian, of Roscoff.

Subsequent civil registrations in Roscoff show that the happy couple had three daughters, Marie Reine, born the 5th of November, 1810; Victoire Catherine Emilie, born the 8th of February 1812; and Suzanne Claire Guillemette, born the 2nd of May 1814.

In most cases of identification through documents, signatures are helpful. The Roscoff registrations offer three versions of Robert Johnson's signature (he was away at sea when Victoire was born).

Sadly, Robert Johnson was lost at sea in 1817. His wife, Suzanne had to go before the Tribunal in Morlaix and have him declared legally dead. The entire judgement was copied into the death register, with much detail. As the shipmaster working for ship owner, Hilary Boucaut, he had sailed the sloop, *Dowe* of Guernsey for England on the

---

[26] AD Finistère, 3 E 295/24, *Roscoff, Actes d'état civil, Mariages An XI-1812* [Roscoff, Civil registrations, Marriages Year 11 to 1812], 24 July 1809, Johnson-Bian Marriage. www.archives-finistere.fr (Accessed 28 August 2020)

first of December. A few days later, wreckage washed ashore near Locquirec, to the north, but all hands were lost. The entry and judgement go for three and a half pages.[27]

It is most likely that Robert Johnson's family knew where he was but, unless hitherto unknown letters or diaries survive, it is unlikely that the researcher will find him in North Carolina records after 1809. French records reveal a life and family, as well as how he died.

Finding people in French civil registrations is increasingly easy. Millions of these registrations are online, on the websites of the Departmental Archives or of the Municipal Archives (especially for the major port cities of Brest, Cherbourg, Bordeaux, Saint-Malo, Le Havre, etc.). These may be accessed free of charge but the websites are entirely in French, of course. In addition to the port cities, if there is reason to suspect that a mariner may have been a prisoner in Napoleonic France and died in prison, his death will have been recorded in the death registrations of the main cities where American seamen were held: Arras, Cambray, Valenciennes and Verdun. Mariners who may have married or died in any of the French colonies around the world can be sought in the civil registers for those territories on the website of the National Overseas Archives, *Archives nationales d'oute-mer* (ANOM).
(http://anom.archivesnationales.culture.gouv.fr/caomec2/)

French commercial genealogy websites, which charge a fee, have some civil registrations. The value of Filae.com or Geneanet.org is that what they do have is indexed but, recalling that neither has all of the country's registrations, a negative result for a search could mean either that the mariner was not in France or that he may have been but the commercial websites do not have the relevant civil registration collection on their websites.[28]

---

[27] AD Finistère, 3 E 295/25, *Roscoff, Actes d'état civil, Décès 1813-1822* [Roscoff, Civil registrations, Deaths 1813-1822], 18 May 1820, Johnson death judgment. www.archives-finistere.fr (Accessed 28 August 2020)

[28] For a full explanation on how to research French civil registrations and to understand them, please see the book, *French Genealogy From Afar*, by the author.

French Naval Records

Since 1668, the French Navy, the *Marine,* has had its own system of drafting men into service, separate from that of the Army. It was compulsory, with most of the men coming from coastal areas. It was devised to ensure a constant supply of men for the navy and to obviate the need for hunting men down and impressing them into naval service. This system of maritime enrollment, *inscription maritime*, functioned through the nineteenth century. Thus, it was rare for captured men to have been forced into service on a French naval vessel.

Nevertheless, French prisoner of war records show that at least a dozen American seamen claimed to have been forced into service in the French Navy. Once again, one must know the name of the vessel, the military port to which it belonged, and the approximate date when the man was on board in order to search for him on a crew list, *role d'équipage*.

Naval crew lists can be found in the *Marine* archives at the branches of the *Service Historique de la Défense* (SHD) at Cherbourg, Brest, Rochefort and Toulon. (Those at Lorient were completely destroyed during the Allied Bombing of Normandy in World War II.)

Many of the principles and avenues of research given above for France are applicable in the other European ports where American seamen could be found, especially: Amsterdam, Antwerp (where a large number of American seamen were imprisoned), Rotterdam, Bergen, Hamburg, Cadiz, Toulon, Marseille, Livorno (Leghorn) and Genoa.

BRITISH DOCUMENTATION

"AFTER A BRITISH LIEUTENANT HAD PICKED THE BEST OF HER CREW"

During the period after American independence, American mariners (some of whom were old enough to have been British before independence) continued to sail to the ports they knew and for the captains and companies they knew, both American and British. The custom of captains abandoning crew in port when they were sick (most often in Liverpool on the British side), or of not employing them for the return voyage meant that the American seaman had to find work on whatever vessel he could in order to get back home.

Working on a British vessel involved him much more directly in the European wars and increased the likelihood that he would be perceived as British by that country's enemies and treated as such, possibly becoming a prisoner of war in France or elsewhere. It also increased the possibility of being impressed, as press gangs prowled port cities such as London and Liverpool, kidnapping any healthy-looking men

---

[29] Abbot, Willis J., *American Merchant Ships and Sailors*. (New York : Dodd, Mead, 1902), 18, illustration. Digitized on the Internet archive. https://archive.org/details/americanmerchant00abboiala/page/84/mode/2up (Accessed 19 August 2020)

and, especially, any experienced seamen. Once the War of 1812 began, Royal Navy vessels attacked and captured American vessels, particularly privateers, and recaptured many of their prizes, making all of the American crew prisoners of war in Britain.

In British records, as elsewhere, the research procedure must still begin with following the vessel and then of finding the man. Where, as with the prisoners of the War of 1812, commercial data bases have indexed prisoner lists, making it possible to search on a man's name, knowing his vessel will help to distinguish him from others with the same or similar names.

British Prize Records or Prize Cases

An enormous number of these have survived. They are not online but can readily be seen at the British National Archives at Kew (TNA) (https://www.nationalarchives.gov.uk/) and copies may be ordered online. They contain, at the very minimum:

- The name of the prize (captured) vessel
- The captain's or master's name
- The name of the capturing vessel
- The capturing captain's name
- Affidavits from the crew of either the capturing vessel or the prize vessel giving very precise details about the capture

British prize case files can contain a great deal of the captured vessel's documentation, including crew lists, cargo manifests, and all kinds of vessel registration and personal papers. (In one docket were found the personal expenses of the shipmaster, a man from Rhode Island, with a description of a new suit of clothes bought before he was captured.)

Below are pages from the prize file describing the capture of the American privateer of the War of 1812, the *Teazer*.[30]

---

[30] TNA, HCA 32/1323/1943, *Records of the High Court of Admiralty and colonial Vice-Admiralty courts, High Court of Admiralty: Prize Court: Papers, Captured Ship: Teazer (master Johnson)*. 28 January 1814. (Photograph by the author)

Hand James Ledfoard for the
American Privateer Frazer of 2 Guns
and 5: other light day [illegible] damage

These are to certify the Commissioners of
the Sixty Navy that Richard Johnson
late Commander of the American Pvt
Privateer Frazer, John H. Culligan late
Lieutenant of D° and James Reynolds
late Lieut of D° Personally Appeared
before me the Hon.ble John Van [illegible]
Esquire Mayor of the Town of S.t George
in the Island of Bermuda, and being
duly sworn on the Holy Evangelists
did severally depose and swear as follows

That on the twenty sixth day of
Nov.r in this present year of our Lord
one thousand eight hundred and twelve
the Schooner Frazer was duly and
regularly commissioned at the City of
Washington by James Madison President
of the United States of America as a
Private armed Schooner of War

That the said Schooner was outfitted
at New York in the United States in
all respects as a Private Ship of War
mounting ten carriage guns with
small arms and all other Weapons
suitable for a Ship of War of that
Description having also a proper
Quantity of Ball Powder and all
other

their necessary Stores Ammunition on Board. That the three Schedules and hold their Appointments on board the said Privateer as is expressed against their respective Names.

That the said Privateer commissioned and fitted for War as before stated being upon the High Seas was met with on the Sixteenth day of December in the present year 1812 in Latitude 35.40 North Longitude 63.40 West by the British Ship of War San Domingo Charles Gill Esq: Captain and was on the same day captured and seized as a Prize by His Majesty's said Ship of War and was immediately burnt and Destroyed.

That when the said Schooner Teazer was first chased by the said Ship of War there were Fifty one Men in Number including Officers and every Description of Persons composing the Crew then serving on board of and belonging to the said Schooner all of whom Surrendered and were taken Prisoners of War by His Majesty's said Ship San Domingo.

And further that this is the first Port within His Majesty's Dominions they have arrived at since their Capture as aforesaid.

The account states that the *Teazer,* an "American schooner privateer", was fitted out in New York, and carried a "privateer commission"; that her commander was Frederick Johnson, with John H. Calligan and James Reynolds as lieutenants, all present giving evidence to the mayor of the town of St. George on Bermuda. They reported that, on the 16th of December 1812, on the high seas, off Bermuda, the *Teazer* encountered the HMS *San Domingo,* Captain Charles Gill, and was captured, "and was immediately burnt and destroyed". All fifty-one officers and crew surrendered and were taken prisoner. The date of the account is the 22nd of December 1812. (As can be seen, this first-hand account differs on some key points with the Wikipedia article on the *Teazer*, taken from an 1899 classic that is riddled with errors.[31]) Other than the officers, the crew are not named and the captors did not bother much with the ship's papers or a crew list before they torched the prize for there are none in the prize case docket. The crew were taken to England as prisoners of war.

British Records of Prisoners of the War of 1812

In the period of the Napoleonic Wars before the War of 1812, if the British found American seamen on the crew of a vessel of French or of another European nationality allied with the French, the men were impressed then and there into the Royal Navy. (Though at least one American convinced his captors that he was French and so, instead of being impressed into a naval ship, was sent to a prison in Britain, from which he promptly escaped.)

Only when war was declared were the American seamen captured on American vessels no longer impressed but sent to prisons in Britain. As noted above, at this time, word of the declaration of war in 1812 flew around the Royal Navy's vessels across the globe and soon, nearly all American seamen who had been impressed declared that they could not be forced to serve their country's enemy. The account of Joseph Furness, of Marblehead, survives. He had been on the crew of the *Dolphin*, out of Salem, when she was captured by a British vessel in August of 1812. He was then

---

[31] Maclay, Edgar Stanton, *A History of American Privateers*. (New York: D. Appleton, 1899).

"carried on board the ship *San Domingo*, where an attempt was made to impress him into the British naval service. With manly heroism, Furness declared that he would not fight against his country, and told his captors to shoot him as he stood, if they chose to do so."[32]

Hundreds of impressed American seamen making similar declarations were shipped from Royal Navy vessels directly to British prisons. Whether captured or "surrendered" on board a Royal Navy vessel, they all were entered into the prisoner registers.

The prison registers are online on two commercial websites. The first is British Online Archives, in the collection entitled "American prisoners of war, 1812-1815" (https://microform.digital/boa/collections/58/american-prisoners-of-war-1812-1815).

It is a cumbersome website to use. One must know the date of capture and the place where the man was first registered as a prisoner of war, e.g. Chatham, Plymouth, etc..

Seeking the men of the *Teazer*, described above as captured off Bermuda in December 1812, one can find the list of the crew as prisoners in the register entitled "Ships and Depots in Overseas Locations - Bermuda, 1812-1815"[33].

---

[32] Roades, Samuel, Jr., *The History and Traditions of Marblehead*, (Boston : Houghton, Osgood, 1880), 243.
https://archive.org/details/historytradition00road/page/242/mode/2up (Accessed 26 September 2020)

[33] "American Prisoners of War, 1812-1815, Ships and Depots in Overseas Locations - Bermuda, 1812-1815", *British Online Archives*, folio 58. https://microform.digital/boa/collections/58/american-prisoners-of-war-1812-1815 (Accessed 29 August 2020) The image has been cropped with Photoshop for the sake of space.

Americans

Current Number	By what Ship, or how taken	Time when		Place where	Name of Prize	Whether Ship of War, Privateer, or Merchant Vessel	Prisoners' Names
		Day	Month	Year			
450	HMS Frolic 3 Remings	16			George Boys Priv'r		Fredrick Johnson
		"					John Mulligan
		"					James Reynolds
		"					Abner Bartlett
		"					Abner K. Draper
		"					Peter Forbes
455		"					Anthony H. Nales

Bermuda

Quality	Time when received into Custody			From what Ship, or whence received	Exchanged, Discharged, Died, or Escaped	Time when			Whither, and by what Order, or Number of Re-entry
	Day	Month	Year			Day	Month	Year	
Capt. 31				HMS Remings 3	D	7 Aug		1813	British Head Quarters
L.b.				"	D	"			"
Sea.				"	D	"			"
D°				"	D	"			"
D°				"	D	"			"
Surgeon				"	D	"			"
Master				"	D	"			"

The list of men continues for two more pages. The details are:

- They were captured by the HMS *San Domingo*
- The capture was on the 16th of December 1812
- The place of capture was at sea
- The name of the prize was *Teazer*, a schooner
- The vessel was sailing as a privateer
- Each man's full name and rank or quality are given
- The date when the man was taken into the custody of the prison (here, the 21st of December)
- What vessel brought him in (here, the same as made the capture)
- What happened to him, whether he was Exchanged (E or Ex), Discharged into another ship (D), died (DD) or Escaped (Esc)
- Date of the above event
- Where he was sent

All were discharged onto a cartel, the *Bostock*, bound for New York, on the 27th of January 1813.

The second online resource for prisoner of war registers is Find My Past (https://www.findmypast.co.uk/) which is much, much easier to use. The following example[34] shows American seamen who had been impressed or captured or "sent into prison by his own request" (that is, refused to serve on an enemy vessel) and sent to Dartmoor prison.

---

[34] "Prisoners of War 1715-1945, Napoleonic Wars, Dartmoor Prison", *Find My Past,* folio 121, left hand page, partial. https://www.findmypast.co.uk/ (Accessed 29 August 2020)

Number	By what Ship, or how taken	Time when	Place where	Name of Prize	Whether Ship of War, Privateer or Merchant Vessel	Prisoners' Names	Quality	Time when received into Custody	From what Ship, or whence received		Place of Nativity	Age	Stature	Person
1001	Amazon	6 Sept	at Largent			Chas. Davey	Seaman	Portsmth. Prison			St. John N.B.	33	5-5	
2	Britain	5 Aug 13		Lyen	Privateer	Jno. Coleman	D.B.				Boston	32	5-4	
3	Act. not known by his own Report					Lewis Cooper	A.B.				Kimbolton	45	5-4	
4	Amazon	Commission granted the 8 Aug.					A.B.							

- Charles Davey, of New Orleans, was impressed at Liverpool
- William Coleman, of Salem, was a seaman on the *Lyon* when she was captured by the *Brilliant*.
- Tannuks (?) Coopor, of Baltimore, was a seaman who had been sent to prison at his own request
- William Simons, of Nantucket, had been impressed into the *Sherebrook*, then was taken out and sent to prison

These prisoner of war registers are a wonderful resource, giving for each man:

- His name
- The date of his capture
- The name of the ship from which taken
- The name of the capturing vessel
- His place of origin
- His physical description, including scars and tattoos
- The prison to which he was sent
- The date of his transfer or release, or death

Royal Navy Muster Rolls and Pay Lists

It can be quite difficult to use these lists to identify with any certainty an American seaman of this period. Mariners of the day told of being impressed into a Royal Navy vessel and of various actions being taken by their captors to obscure the Americans' identity and nationality. These include:

- Seaman's Protection Certificates and any other documents sometimes were torn up and thrown into the sea
- On the muster and pay lists:
    - Americans were given false birthplaces in Britain instead of the true ones in the United States
    - Americans were registered under the names of dead British crew members
    - Many men were listed merely by name, with no details at all

Yet, there were some cases where they were entered honestly, with their true names and places of birth, and with the fact that they were impressed noted as well. In most cases, further, corroborating documentation will be needed in order to be certain of a man's identification.

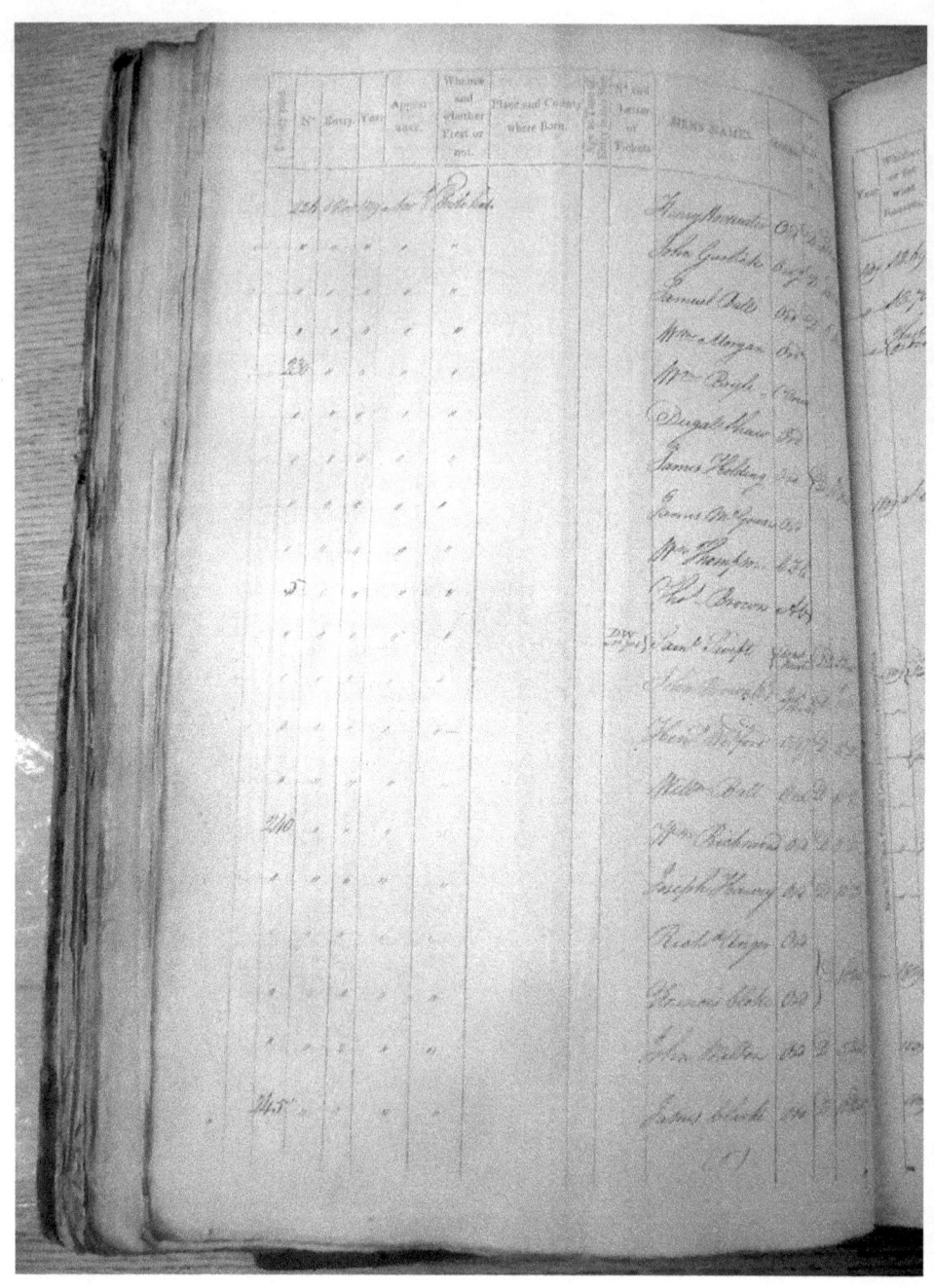

The example above[35] shows a nearly empty roll from the HMS *Manilla*. The column headings for the left-hand page are:

- Bounty paid
- Entry [into the Navy]
- Year
- Appearance [on the vessel]
- Whence and whether prest [pressed or impressed]
- Place and county where born
- Age at Time of Entry in this Ship
- Number and Letter of Tickets
- Men's Names
- Quality [rank]
- D, DD or R [Discharged, Dead or Run away]
- Time of Discharge

All of the names on the page are dittoed as having come to the *Manilla* from the "HMS *Thisbe* late" on the 8th of November 1809. With a page such as this, one would have to search through the whole book as well as those coming earlier or later to find an entry with more detail. It can be a few hours in the archives, but the search can be fruitful. Below shows part of another page in the same book[36], showing more detail for each man:

---

[35] TNA, ADM 37/2602, *Records of the Admiralty, Naval Forces, Royal Marines, Coastguard, and related bodies, Admiralty: Ships' Musters (Series II) Ship: Manilla)*, 1809 Oct - 1810 July. Page/folio not numbered. (Photograph by Nicola Scott-Francis)
[36] Ibid.

Bounty pay Do W Thomas	Sealed Religious	38	John Gale	Boatswain (mate)
	Philadelphia			
"	Charlotte of Jamaica	22	James Lewis	Copr 66.3
"	Baton Mountain			
"	Leith	31	So Mustead	AB
"	England			
"	Liverpool	70	Thomas Goodard	AB
	(France)			
5 "	Philadelphia Dunkirk	45	John Brown	S.B & Mask
"	Newcastle	75	Chr Brown	AB
	upon Tyne			
"	Leverpool	57	Nich Osgood	AB
	Portugal			Own Request
"	Richmond	24	Isaac Parent	Jaler
"	New York	20	John Horwalu	AB
	Pensylvania			

The last fully visible name, Henry Hornewater, is also the first name on the earlier shown page. Here, more detail is given. He was transferred from the "*Thisbe* late *Latona*", he was aged twenty-two, from New York in America. A bit of research (online but also and especially in Rif Winfield's *British Warships in the Age of Sail, 1793-1817*) shows that the HMS *Thisbe*, *Latona* and *Manilla* all were off Portugal in late 1809. So, "*Thisbe* late *Latona*" would indicate that these men would have been first on the *Latona*, then loaded onto the *Thisbe*, which then passed them to the *Manilla*. By then, Henry Hornewater appeared as an ordinary seaman on the *Manilla*'s muster.

Finding Royal Navy muster rolls and pay lists requires that, as always, one knows the name of the vessel, or at least one of the vessels, on which the man served in the Royal Navy and the approximate date when he was on board. The records of the National Archives of Great Britain (TNA) can be searched on the TNA website to know if those books for that vessel for that time have survived (many did not). The muster roll books are massive and, though one may order copies, it can be quite expensive to have copied an entire book or even a year's pages within a book. If it is not possible to go to Kew to do this research, it is best to hire an experienced naval researcher to do so. (Beware, many generalist genealogists or researchers without naval research experience do not understand these books and leave out crucial information.)

Find My Past, in the series "British Royal Navy, Ships' Musters" (which is within the category of "Regimental & Service Records in Military, armed forces & conflict") has the muster rolls of a few vessels, but almost none of the early nineteenth century. It is a good idea to check their list of ships' names first.

If there may be a chance that an American mariner remained in the Royal Navy (and some did), it is then worth pursuing him further in Royal Navy records. The following guides are helpful for such research.

- A comprehensive list of all online resources concerning the Royal Navy, can be found on the resources page of the National Museum of the Royal Navy.
  (https://www.nmrn.org.uk/research/online-resources)
- Scott, Jonathan, "The 14 best websites for Royal Navy family history", *Who Do You Think You Are? Magazine*, December 2019

CONCLUSION

This booklet and its presentation of resources has a quite narrow focus on finding and identifying American merchant mariners of the early nineteenth century. As such, its readership will be less the historian, who looks more at groups within societies, and more the family historian or the biographer, who look for as much facts and information as possible about specific individuals.

The research is not easy and is not always possible online but, as the case studies that follow show, it is possible to find an American merchant seaman in documentation across the world and to reconstruct, if not his life, at least a part of his career.

CASE STUDY

A SEAMAN FROM MARBLEHEAD, CAPTURED ON A FRENCH PRIVATEER, JOINS THE ROYAL NAVY

American Documentation

Ambrose Dodd was baptized on the 12th of June 1768 in Marblehead, Massachusetts, the son of Ambrose Dodd and his wife Mary Homan.[37] It would seem that his father died in the next few years, for, in 1771, Mary Dodd married Simon Elliott in Marblehead.[38] In 1786, at the age of eighteen, young Ambrose married Elizabeth Grow, and was the father of Betsy, baptized in 1787, of Sally, baptized in 1789, and of Ambrose, baptized in 1791, all in Marblehead.[39] He then disappears from the Massachusetts public records.

Published American Sources

Nothing in the records indicated that he was a seaman but, on the 8th of August 1809, the New York *Evening Post* published a "List of American Sailors, detained as prisoners of War in France" that included "Ambrose Dodd, of Marblehead" as a prisoner held at the depot in Sarre-Libre.[40] Four years later, the Massachusetts House of Representatives Committee on Impressed Seamen received as evidence fifty-one depositions from mariners, ship owners, merchants and others containing the names of American seamen who had been impressed by the British. The deposition of William Storey states that a number of men from Marblehead, including Ambrose Dodd, had been "absent for several years" and "that their friends had ascertained them to be under

---

[37] "Massachusetts, Town and Vital Records, 1620-1988" [database on-line], *Ancestry,* https://www.ancestry.com/search/collections/2495/ (Accessed 25July 2020)
[38] Ibid.
[39] Ibid.
[40] *The Evening Post*, New York. 8 August 1809, p.2, col. 5. https://www.newspapers.com/newspage/33462012/ (Accessed 3 September 2020)

impressment."[41] No further mention of him that is not a repetition of the latter publication could be found.

Based on the paucity of documentation, one might have thought that Ambrose Dodd died in a French prison or from the brutalities of impressment or was simply "lost at sea". Though his ultimate end could not be discovered, French prisoner of war records and British Royal Navy musters reveal a long, war-time section of his life.

Published British Sources

In July of 1803, *Lloyds List* reported that the British merchant vessel, *Rachael*, captain Cooper, on a voyage from Nevis, in the Caribbean, to Bristol, was captured by a French privateer out of Lorient, the *Agile*, off Cape Clear, an island of the southwestern tip of Ireland.[42] The capture was also reported in the *Journal de Paris* on the 20th of July.

> "Yesterday morning, the privateer *Agile*, armed twenty days ago, returned to this port after a happy cruise. On the 4th [of the Republican month of messidor] she took the English brig, Valentine…of Bristol, with a crew of nine men. On the 6th, she took the English ship, *Augusta*, from Antibes for London, about 400 tons, carrying sugar and coffee, and with a crew of sixteen men. On the 9th, she took the English ship Rachel, coming from Nevis…about 300 tons, carrying sugar and coffee, going to Bristol, and with a crew of ten men."[43]

As was the usual procedure at the time, the crew of the victim vessel, with Ambrose Dodd amongst them, were removed and taken onto the predator vessel, becoming prisoners of war. Some of the *Agile*'s crew, forming a "prize crew" replaced them. Their goal was to sail the prize

---

[41] Massachusetts. General Court. House of Representatives. Committee on Impressed Seamen. *Report of the Committee of the House of representatives of Massachusetts, on the subject of impressed seamen: with the evidence and documents accompanying it.* Boston : Russell and Cutler, printers, 1813, p.57.
[42] *Lloyd's List*, no. 4367, 15 July 1803, and no. 4368, 19 July 1803. https://tinyurl.com/yxk892bu (Accessed 2 September 2020)
[43] *Journal de Paris*, 1 Thermidor, An XI [20 July 1803], 1803 no. 361, p1923. (Translation by the author.) https://tinyurl.com/yy8vxqfv (Accessed 8 September 2020)

vessel, which was laden with sugar, with all speed to the nearest French port, where the prize could be sold. They did not make it. The *Rachael* was recaptured by a British privateer, the *Swallow*, and taken in to Liverpool;[44] her French crew became prisoners of war in Britain. Had she been recaptured a bit earlier, before the exchange of crews, Ambrose Dodd would not have become a prisoner in France and might have remained undocumented. Were he to have continued his work on the *Rachael*, he might have been on her when she was wrecked in a hurricane at Nevis on the 7th of July 1811.[45]

He was on the *Agile* when she went in to Lorient and dropped off the prisoners. As the *Rachael* had been retaken, there was no prize to judge and no hope of release for the captured crew. Prisoners of war were usually gathered into groups and marched, under guard and often in chains, to a prison depot in the interior. Ambrose Dodd would have been marched from Lorient to Rennes, thence to the region north of Paris, through Château-Thierry, and finally, to Epinal, nearly eight hundred kilometers in the summer heat. Dodd was at the time about thirty-five years old and probably reasonably fit, but such a march would have taken its toll on him.

American Manuscript Collections

On the 11th of August, from Château-Thierry, he wrote to the United States' Consul General in Paris, Fulwar Skipwith, begging for help and explaining his case.

> "I address myself to you that I may be claimed and taken from the Prison of Epinal in Lorraine whither I am thus far in the road to be conducted thither, being taken aboard an English Merchantman named the Racheal Bound to Bristol and I was carried into Lorient, having engaged in this vessel the homeward bound passage from St. Kits without having any knowledge of the War. My name is Ambrose Dodd. Born in Marble Head near Boston & out of which port I served my time

---

[44] *The Morning Post*. London, England. 18 July 1803.
https://tinyurl.com/y4sy82ar (Accessed 2 September 2020)
[45] Farr, Grahame E. editor, *Records of Bristol Ships, 1800-1838 (Vessels over 150 tons)*, (Publications of the Bristol Record Society Vol XV. Bristol : Bristol Record Society, 1950), 247.

with my Stepfather named Elliot in the Employ of Capt. Foster. My stepfather's uncle Simon Elliot keeps a Tobacco and Snuff Shop at Boston. I am without any Papers notwithstanding I hope after the Explanations I have here given and the inquiries you may make thereupon that you will be so kind as to make use of your Power and influence to procure my Liberty and be so good as to advise me of the Same..."[46]

Further on in the same letter, in a brief biographical note, he added that his:

"Protection [Certificate] was unfortunately left in his chest is signed by Mr. Fox, Consul at Falmouth in February 1794. Belonged at that time to the Brig *Sea Nymph*, Captn John Peyton, of Philadelphia, belonging to Mr. Lyme..."

French Documentation

He was not released. It is almost certain that this was because he was on the crew of an enemy vessel. Even though he was an American and thus of a neutral nationality, because he was "aiding the enemy", the French authorities would not have released him. He may have tried to escape or been fractious, for he next appears on a list of American prisoners that was made in 1807 that showed him at the prison depot in Bitche, the high-security, brutally run prison where troublesome prisoners were sent. To the interlocutor making the list, Dodd changed his story and stated that, in about 1801, he "shipped out of Boston, under Captain Foster." He said he was impressed by the English that year and "put aboard the British ship, *Rachel*, of Bristol, bound for the West Indies."[47]

This is clearly not true. The Royal Navy never put men on merchant ships. The French at that time did accept that Americans prisoners of war who had been captured from Royal Navy ships might have been forced into that service. When the men could prove that they had been

---

[46] Library of Congress, Manuscript Division, Causten-Pickett Papers, 1765-1916, carton 14, Ambrose Dodd and others to Fulwar Skipwith, Library of Congress, Washington, DC.
[47] SHD Vincennes, Yj19, *Prisonniers de guerre anglais* [English prisoners of war] 1807, Census of American prisoners.

impressed and, thus, were not willingly aiding the enemy, the French authorities released them from prison. Once the American prisoners discovered this, many claimed to have been impressed. However, it was very difficult to prove. Though Skipwith wrote to Talleyrand, the Minister of External Relations, about Dodd and others, trying to negotiate their release because they were American, not British, seamen and had been "forced to work" on British ships,[48] he was not able to prove this to the satisfaction of the French. In 1809, after six years, Ambrose Dodd was still a prisoner in France.

That year, he, with about a dozen other American seamen, signed up to work on the French privateer, *Etoile no. 2*.[49] To leave prison temporarily in order to fight the enemy on a French privateer was something permitted only to prisoners of neutral nationality. The French Minister for War allowed ship owners to visit prisons to recruit prisoners for this. The fact that Ambrose Dodd was able to do this shows that his nationality as an American had been accepted by the French authorities but had not won him his freedom. Two months later, he was on the French privateer named *Etoile no. 2*, a lugger of fourteen guns, when she was captured by HMS *Euryalus*.[50] The crew became prisoners of war of the British. The French men on the crew were sent to Portsmouth and appear on the reception roster.[51] The Americans, including Ambrose Dodd, remained on the HMS *Euryalus*.

British Documentation

On the 6th of November 1809, he appears on the *Euryalus* list of "Supernumeraries, for victuals only" as "Ambrose Dodd of

---

[48] SHD Vincennes, Yj29, *Prisonniers de guerre anglai;* [English prisoners of war].
[49] SHD Vincennes, FF2/104, *Guerre de l'an II : Prisonniers neutres embarqués sur les corsaires;* [War of Year II: Neutral prisoners embarked on privateers] folio 10.
[50] *The London Gazette,* no. 16315, 14 November 1809, p. 1826. https://www.thegazette.co.uk/London/issue/16315/page/1826. (Accessed 2 September 2020)
[51] "Prisoners of War 1715-1945 Napoleonic Wars," ADM 103/379, *Find My Past,* https://tinyurl.com/ydesrlbh. (Accessed 2 September 2020)

Marblehead [aged] 42, able seaman."[52]. The next day, he and the other Americans appear on the muster list of the *Euryalus*, "having no doubt understood the options open to them: to be incarcerated with the French POWs or incarcerated with British tars."[53] Being rated as an able seaman on the muster meant that Dodd was recognized to have extensive seafaring experience and skill; this was the second time that it enabled him to exchange prison for the sea.

Dodd remained aboard the HMS *Euryalus* for nearly five years, appearing consistently on the pay book as either "Sail Maker's Mate" or "Quarter Master's Mate", until the 21st of May 1814, when he was discharged to the HMS *Rivoli*.[54] During his time on board, the *Euryalus* was stationed in the Mediterranean. While there, in 1811 and 1813, she captured two French privateers and Dodd would have had his tiny share in the prize money. He would have taken part in the attack by the *Euryalus* on a French convoy in 1813 that destroyed twenty-two vessels, and he was on the ship, under quarantine (indicating that the vessel had visited a port, probably in North Africa, where there was a plague outbreak), in Marseilles, when the news went round the world that Napoleon had been defeated in April 1814.[55]

At the same time, Britain was also at war with Dodd's own country; the War of 1812 was at its peak. A month after Dodd was transferred from the *Euryalus* to the *Rivoli*, the *Euryalus* sailed for Chesapeake Bay and then up the Potomac to bombard Washington, D.C., making the reason for his discharge clear: he might have been willing to fight for his country's enemy but perhaps would not go so far as to fight against his own country, or perhaps the captain transferred all Americans off the *Euryalus* as a precaution.

---

[52] TNA, ADM 37/1221, *Records of the Admiralty, Naval Forces, Royal Marines, Coastguard, and related bodies, Admiralty: Ships' Musters (Series II) Ship: Euryalus*; 1809, May-Dec.
[53] Brian Cooper, researcher of British prisoners of the Napoleonic Wars.
[54] TNA, ADM 35/3443, *Records of the Admiralty, Naval Forces, Royal Marines, Coastguard, and related bodies, Admiralty: Ships' Pay Books, Ship: Euryalus*; 1809 Oct.1 – 1815 Aug. 29.
[55] Paul Benyon, "Index of 19th Century Naval Vessels and some of their movements", *Naval Social History - Circa 1793 - 1920+, Rootsweb* https://sites.rootsweb.com/~pbtyc/18-1900/E/01681.html (Accessed 12 September 2020)

Though Britain was still at war with the United States, in Europe, the wars, at last, were over. Financially exhausted, the Royal Navy immediately after the defeat of France, began to discharge seamen and to sell off ships. Ambrose Dodd was discharged from the HMS *Rivoli* to the HMS *Swiftsure* "for a passage to England", calling at Malta.[56] He was at last released from the Royal Navy at Portsmouth Dockyard on the 10th of September 1814.

As he stepped off the *Swiftsure*, he would have had in his pocket his pay for his five years' service. He was about forty-six years old and would have been away from Marblehead for at least eleven years, if not more. The United States and Britain were still at war in September of 1814, so it was unlikely (but not impossible) that he would have found an American ship in the harbor to take him home. No record of his return to the United States or of his death there has been found, though he may have gone back. The name, Ambrose Dodd, was common in Britain in the nineteenth century and there are a few marriage and death records of men with the name. Perhaps one concerns the man from Marblehead who was a merchant seaman on American vessels from at least 1794 to 1803, a prisoner of war in France from 1803 to 1809, and on the musters of the British Royal Navy from 1809 to 1814.

---

[56] "Prisoners of War 1715-1945, Napoleonic Wars" ADM 37/5142, 37/4146, and 37/5158, *Find My Past*, https://tinyurl.com/ydesrlbh (Accessed 2 September 2020)

CASE STUDY

A NANTUCKET WHALER DIES IN A FRENCH PRISON

Peleg Bunker was a Quaker from Nantucket and one of the whalers who worked for William Rotch. He is not obscure, so mentions of him in published works appear on Internet searches, including but not limited to the following:

Published Sources

- *Nantucket Doorways* by Edward A. Stackpole and Christopher B. Summerfield, 1992
- *Why Nantucket Quakers?* by Robert J. Leach and Willard C. Heiss, 1979
- *The History of Nantucket: county, island, and town, including...* by Alexander Starbuck, 1969
- *Catalogue of Nantucket Whalers: and Their Voyages from 1815 to 1870*, Hussey & Robinson, printers, 1876
- *Whales and Destiny: the Rivalry Between America, France and Britain...* by Edward A. Stackpole, 1972
- *Les Baleiniers français, de Louis XVI à Napoléon* by Thierry Du Pasquier, 1990
- *Ships Employed in the South Sea Whale Fishery from Britain: 1775-1815...* by Jane M. Clayton, 2014.

American Documentation

- Edward A. Stackpole Collection, 1750-1990
  (the author of two of the above books)
  Manuscripts Collection
  Research Library & Archives
  Nantucket Historical Association

The main source for biographical information is the "sketch" of his life by Peleg Bunker's great-granddaughter, Lydia Bunker Gardner. However, the letters from Peleg are her copies and the account of his capture by the French is hers, as told to her and written many years after the fact.

Lydia Bunker Gardner wrote in her sketch that:

- Peleg Bunker was a whaling captain from Nantucket
- During the American Revolution, Bunker took his family to New York state, and returned to Nantucket and to whaling when the war ended
- He then worked for William Rotch in London
- During the Napoleonic Wars, while sailing the *Falkland*, an English whaler, Bunker was "captured in the English Channel by the French"
- He was marched to Verdun prisoner of war camp with the *Falkland*'s officers and men
- He spent five years in the camp
- The United States government made "every effort...for their release"
- "Appeals were sent to Bonaparte from the Friends Society, of which Peleg Bunker was a member" for his release
- Upon receiving the news of his release, "the joy of it... was too much for Peleg Bunker...and he died instantly...."

The copied letters, one to Peleg's wife and one to an unnamed son, are dated 1805 and 1806; both are from Verdun.[57] They mention:

- A Christopher Bunker who had been in hospital but was recovered and returned to prison
- That Peleg had received two letters from his sons, Obed and Tristan
- That Benjamin Hussey in Dunkirk was the person through whom Peleg's wife could send letters to him

This is a lovely summary of his life, career, capture and death and it is the source used by the authors of some of the published materials that mention Peleg Bunker. However, as will be seen, there are a few discrepancies.

Among the microfilmed Diplomatic Dispatches from Paris, are found copies of letters from Peleg Bunker himself, asking the

---

[57] Nantucket Historical Association, Research Library & Archives, Manuscripts Collection, Edward A. Stackpole Collection, 1750-1990.

American Minister to France to intercede on his behalf. In one letter[58], Bunker states that:

- He arrived in England from America during the Peace [of Amiens, 1802-3]
- The ship he had arrived on was sold [leaving him with no return voyage]
- He took a job as Chief Mate on an English ship sailing to the South Seas
- During the voyage, the Master died and he assumed command
- He was captured on the return voyage as his ship was entering the English Channel, by the French privateer, the *Vaillant*, of Bordeaux
- He encloses a notarized copy of his Seaman's Protection Certificate by way of proof of his American nationality [not microfilmed at this point but later]

Captain Bunker is bending the truth a bit here, as we shall see. He implies that he was a mate and seaman, when he had been a master for some years. He implies that he had simply taken a job on an English vessel when he had been sailing for Rotch's English whaling companies exclusively for at least ten years. It is true that the master on his vessel died and he assumed command, and it is true that his ship was captured by the *Vaillant*.

It is apparent that the Minister in Paris, Robert R. Livingston, wrote to the French authorities claiming Peleg Bunker as an American citizen who should be released, for the reply, dated the 30th of April, appears in the dispatches. The Director of Administration in the Ministry of War wrote to Livingston:

"As Captain Bunker...was taken while sailing under the British flag and in the service of England, it is the intention of the First

---

[58] Peleg Bunker to U.S. Minister to France, Letter, 4 March 1804; Vol. 9, 26 December 1803-23 October 1804; *Despatches from U.S. Ministers to France, 1789-1906*, (National Archives Microfilm Publication M34, roll 5); Record Group 59: General Records of the Department of State, U.S. National Archives.

Consul [Napoleon] that he be considered as a prisoner of war."⁵⁹

From this, it would appear that Peleg's great-granddaughter was mistaken that he died of joy at having been released.

British Documentation

Though American by birth, since Bunker was sailing a British vessel, he was considered to be a British prisoner of war by the French. He was also considered to be one of their own by the British, and he appears as such in some British documentation. The *Times* newspaper included him in a list of "English Prisoners in France", published on the 5th of June 1804.⁶⁰ The list was not of seamen but only masters of British vessels who were alive and well in French prisons. It named him as "P. Bunker, master of the vessel *William Bruce*, of London" (not the *Falkland*. In fact, no *Falkland* appears on the list.)

The Admiralty received regular reports from the French about the deaths of British prisoners of war. These are available on Find My Past. A page from Verdun lists Peleg Bunker, *capitaine marchand*, or captain in the merchant marine, as having died there on the 24th or 25th of February 1806.⁶¹

French Documentation

As might be expected, the French had a great deal of documentation on Peleg Bunker and on the capture of his vessel. Firstly, the naval records in the *Archives de la Marine* (SHD) record the captures by the *Vaillant,* in a large table of privateers sent out from Bordeaux

---

[59] Dejean, Minister of War, to U.S. Minister to France, Letter, 30 April 1804; Vol. 9, 26 December 1803-23 October 1804; *Despatches from U.S. Ministers to France, 1789-1906*, (National Archives Microfilm Publication M34, roll 5); Record Group 59: General Records of the Department of State, U.S. National Archives.
[60] *The Times*, London, England, 5 June 1804, no. 6041, p. 3, col. 3 ; www.newspapers.com/image/32776486 (Accessed 1 February 2020)
[61] *Register of Deaths for British POWs 1794-1814*, ADM 103/631 frame 278, (TNA), www.findmypast.co.uk (Accessed 20 February 2020)

between the month of *prairial An XI and prairial An XIII* [May 1803 to May 1805], detailing their owners, costs and captures, if any.[62]

The table shows that the *Vaillant*, Captain Etienne, captured four English vessels:

- the *William Douglas*
- the *Union*
- the *William Bruce*
- the *Cleopatra*

This matches the information of the British *Times* list that also gave Peleg Bunker's vessel as the *William Bruce*.

The Ministry of War maintained a file on the prisoner Peleg Bunker,[63] though it contains only six documents, including a French translation of the notarized copy of his Seaman's Protection Certificate.

This translation states that "Captain Peleg Bunker" was:

- Aged forty-seven "December last"
- A native of Cherborn [Sherborne] in the county of Nantucket, Massachusetts
- A subject of the Commonwealth of Massachusetts
- A citizen of the United States of America

It was signed by Abner Coffin [or Coffyn], notary public in Sherborn, on the 27th of April 1795. The other documents in the dossier include a letter from Livingston, requesting Bunker's release, and the Ministry of War memos discussing the negative response.

---

[62] SHD Vincennes, FF2/11, *Armements en Courses, 5e arrondissement, Quartier de Bordeaux* [Arming [vessels] for [privateering] cruises, 5*th* arrondissement, Bordeaux section], *prairial An XI and prairial An XIII* [May 1803 to May 1805].

[63] SHD Vincennes, Yj40, *Archives de la Ministre de Guerre- Prisonniers de guerre anglais* [Archives of the Ministry of War-English Prisoners of War] – Peleg Bunker.

Civil registrations were fairly new in France at that time, having been instituted about fifteen years earlier, but they were thorough. Peleg Bunker's death registration can be found online on the website of the Departmental Archives of Meuse, where Verdun and its prison were located.

While French death registrations almost never give a cause of death, they do give a fair amount of information for the purposes of identification. The death registration[64] states that "Peleg Bunker, English prisoner of war"

- Died on the 24th of February 1806 at Verdun
- Was aged sixty-one
- Was born in "Antiquet" [Nantucket] in America
- Was the spouse of Lydie Gardner
- Was a captain of a merchant vessel

Scattered among the French naval records are various loose lists about the British prisoners of war. One of these, dated 1810, four years after Peleg Bunker died, has his name on it.[65]

It gives his name, date of death, place of birth, profession, all as stated in the other documents. Additionally, it states that his personal effects were given to another prisoner, a Christopher Bunker, who was "a relative".

---

[64] AD Meuse, 2E 558(52); Verdun, *Actes d'état civil, Décès 1806* [Verdun, Civil registrations, Deaths 1806], entry 161, 25 February 1806, Death of Peleg Bunker. www.archives-meuse.fr (Accessed 28 August 2020)
[65] SHD Vincennes, FF2/10; *Archives de la Marine - "Etat des Prisonniers anglaise décédés en France dont les effets ou l'argent ont été remis...."* [Archives of the Navy-List of English prisoners of war who died in France whose effects and money have been returned to...] 1 March 1810.

Selected Bibliography

While there are many books and publications that deal with merchant seamen from the mid-nineteenth century onwards, other than those already mentioned in this work, there are few that cover the men of the early nineteenth century. Thus, the following list (restricted to works in English) is, by necessity, short and includes more general works.

- Anonymous "A Citizen of Baltimore", *Observations on the Impressment of American Seamen by the Officers of Ships of War, and Vessels Commissioned By and Acting Under the Authority of Great Britain; With a Few Remarks on the Doctrine of Non-Expatriation, To Which Is Added, a Correct List of Impressed Seamen, Taken From Documents Laid Before Congress,* (Baltimore : G. Dobbin & Murphy, 1806).
- Bolster, W. Jeffrey, *Black Jacks : African American Seamen in the Age of Sail*, (Cambridge, Massachusetts : Harvard University Press, 1997).
- Bolster, W. Jeffrey, ""To Feel Like a Man" : Black Seamen in the Northern States, 1800-1860", *The Journal of American History*, Vol. 76, No. 4 (Mar., 1990), 1173-1199.
- Brown, Diana and Colin, *The Whaler and the Privateer " the Story of Two Ships, 1795-1807*, (Nantucket : Letter of Marque Press, 1993).
- Choate, Jean, editor, *At Sea Under Impressment : Accounts of Involuntary Service Aboard Navy and Pirate Vessels, 1700-1820*, (Jefferson, North Carolina : McFarland, 1988).
- Clubb, Stephen, "A Journal Containing an account of the wrongs, sufferings, and neglect, experienced by Americans in France. By Stephen Clubb, late a prisoner in that Empire." *The Magazine of History With Notes and Queries*. Extra Numbers, Vol. XIII, comprising Numbers 49-52, (Tarrytown : William Abbatt, 1916), 149-201.
- Creighton, Margaret S., "Fraternity in the American Forecastle, 1830-1870", *The New England Quarterly*, Vol. 63, No. 4 (Dec., 1990), 531-557.
- Crowhurst, Patrick, *The French War on Trade : Privateering 1793-1815*, (Aldershot : Scolar Press, 1989).

- Dixon, Ruth Priest, "Genealogical Fallout from the War of 1812", *Prologue Magazine*, Vol. 24, NO. 4 (Spring 1992), [no page numbers].
- Dana, Richard Henry, Jr., *Two Years Before the Mast, and Twenty-four Years After*, Harvard Classics, Vol. 23, (New York : Collier, 1957).
- Durand, James R. *The Life and Adventures of James R. Durand...*, (Sandwich, Massachusetts : Chapman Billies, 1995).
- Dye, Ira, "Early American Merchant Seafarers", *Proceedings of the American Philosophical Society*, Vol. 120, No. 5 (Oct. 15, 1976), 331-360.
- Esdaile, Charles, *Napoleon's Wars : an International History, 1803-1815*, (London : Penguin Books, 2008).
- Fabel, Robin F.A., "Self-Help in Dartmoor: Black and White Prisoners in the War of 1812", *Journal of the Early Republic*, Vol. 9, No. 2 (Summer, 1989), 165-190.
- Gilje, Paul A., "On the Waterfront: Maritime Workers in New York City in the Early Republic, 1800 –1850", *New York History*, Vol. 77, No. 4 (October 1996), 395-426.
- Gilje, Paul A., *To Swear Like a Sailor : Maritime Culture in America, 1750-1850*, (New York : Cambridge University Press, 2016).
- Head, David, *Privateers of the Americas : Spanish American Privateering from the United States in the Early Republic*, (Athens, Georgia : University of Georgia Press, 2015).
- Hicks, Dan, *True Born Columbians: the Promises and Perils of National Identity for American Seafarers of the Early Republican Period : a Thesis in History*, Pennsylvania State University, Graduate School, College of the Liberal Arts, 2007.
- Langley, Harold D., *Social Reform in the United States Navy, 1798-1862*, (Urbana, Illinois : University of Illinois Press, 1967).
- Lemisch, Jesse, "Jack Tar in the Streets : Merchant Seamen in the Politics of Revolutionary America", *The William and Mary Quarterly*, Vol. 25 No. 3, (July 1968), 371-407.
- Maclay, Edgar Stanton, *A History of American Privateers*, (New York : D. Appleton and Co., 1899).
- Malloy, Mary, *African Americans in the Maritime Trades : A Guide to Resources in New England*, Kendall Whaling Museum

- Monograph Series No. 6 (Stuart M. Frank, Series Editor), Sharon, MA : The Kendall Whaling Museum, 1990.
- Marzagalli, Silvia; Sofka, James R.; McClusker, John, editors, *Rough Waters American Involvement with the Mediterranean in the Eighteenth and Nineteenth Centuries*, Research in Maritime History No. 44, (St. John's Newfoundland, International Maritime Economic History Association, 2010).
- McCarthy, Matthew, *Privateering, Piracy and British ``Policy in Spanish America, 1810-1830*, (Woodbridge, Suffolk : Boydell Press, 2013).
- Paine, Ralph Delahaye, *The Old Merchant Marine – a Chronicle of American Ships and Sailors*, Chronicles of America Series, Vol. 36, (New Haven : Yale University Press, 1919).
- Perl-Rosenthal, Nathan, *Citizen Sailors : Becoming American in the Age of Revolution*, (Cambridge, Massachusetts : Belknap Press, 2015).
- Petrie, David A., *The Prize Game : Lawful Looting on the High Seas in the Days of Fighting Sail*, (New York : Berkley Books, 1990).
- Runyan, Timothy J., editor, *Ships, Seafaring and Society : Essays in Maritime History*, (Detroit : Wayne State University Press, 1987).
- Stackpole, Edouard A., *Whales & Destiny : The Rivalry between America, France, and Britain for Control of the Southern Whale Fishery, 1785-1825*, (University of Massachusetts Press, 1972).
- Tyng, Charles, *Before the Wind : the Memoir of an American Sea Captain, 1808-1833*, (New York : Penguin Books, 1999).
- Vickers, Daniel and Walsh, Vince, *Young Men and the Sea : Yankee Seafarers in the Age of Sail*, (New Haven : Yale University Press, 2005).
- "War of 1812 Papers" of the Department of State, 1789-1815, National Archives Microfilm Publications, Pamphlet Accompanying Microcopy No. 588, Washington, D.C.: National Archives and Records Service, General Services Administration, 1965.
- Zimmerman, James Fulton, *Impressment of American Seamen*, (Port Washington, New York : Kennikat Press, 1966).

Finally, for a full and very thorough survey and explanation of all War of 1812 records concerning American servicemen (not merchant seamen) consider the excellent online course presented by the National Genealogical Society (now part of the Federation of Genealogical Societies), "War of 1812 Records" by David Rencher, CG, Rebecca Koford, CG, Ken Nelson and Michael Hall.
(https://www.ngsgenealogy.org/cgs/war-of-1812-records/)
The course description reads:

"This course helps students understand the various records associated with the War of 1812 and their genealogical significance. Students will increase their understanding of the causes of the War of 1812, the structure of the military, the records kept during the war, and how to use the various records in their family history research.

Students will examine numerous records including Acts of Congress, pension records, compiled military service records, bounty land records, naval and marine corps records, muster rolls, ship's logs, diplomatic records, and state militia records.

The course is divided into fourteen modules, which include readings, web links, self-correcting quizzes, practical assignments, and a reading and reference list. A full syllabus is provided to course registrants."

ACRONYMS FOR ARCHIVES

AD	Archives départementales
AM	Archives municipales
AN	Archives nationales
ANOM	Archives nationales d'outre-mer
SHD	Service Historique de la Défense
TNA	The National Archives (of Great Britain)

www.ingramcontent.com/pod-product-compliance
Lightning Source LLC
LaVergne TN
LVHW041341080426
835512LV00006B/567